The Concept of Polymediality

Marios Joannou Elia

The Concept of Polymediality

Literary Sources as an Inherent Polymedial Element of Music

SCHOTT

Coverstreifen: *Autosymphonic* – Open-air multimedia symphony
(2010–11), 360-degree positioning of musical groups
Quelle: Marios Joannou Elia, m:con – mannheim:congress GmbH

Bibliografische Information der Deutschen Nationalbibliothek

Die Deutsche Nationalbibliothek verzeichnet diese Publikation in
der Deutschen Nationalbibliografie; detaillierte bibliografische
Daten sind im Internet über http://dnb.d-nb.de abrufbar.

978-3-95983-100-0 (Paperback)
978-3-95983-101-7 (Hardcover)

© 2017 Schott Music GmbH & Co. KG, Mainz

Alle Rechte vorbehalten.
Nachdruck in jeder Form sowie die Wiedergabe durch Fernsehen,
Rundfunk, Film, Bild- und Tonträger oder Benutzung für Vorträge,
auch auszugsweise, nur mit Genehmigung des Verlags.

Printed in Germany

Abstract

The commentary focuses on the predominantly applied extraneous media in my music, especially the inclusion of literary sources.

The discourse begins with a succinct description of the concept of polymediality, which involves two dimensions: the work-immanent compositional dimension and polymediality in the process of staging (Chapter I).

Chapter II considers literary sources as a constituent component of music's polymediality. The first part is preoccupied with the implementation of textual elements and vocality in instrumental works, with special reference to the orchestral piece *Akanthai*. Simultaneously, this section elucidates a series of fundamental architectural tools and aspects of the music, encompassing (a) the methodological advancement concerning analogous relationships, (b) the processing of linear transitions and polyphonic settings depending on the model of imitative interaction, (c) the polydimensional articulation of homogeneity, (d) the aspect of permanent fleetingness, (e) the different facets of hybridization and their implications, (f) the question of the musico-literary intermediality form, and (g) the concept of polyaesthetics. To this extent, the commentary reports on research aiming at elaborating the hypothesis that musical and non-musical elements, like literary sources, are mustered from a diversified spectrum of coherent principles.

Turning to the example of the opera *Die Jagd*, the second part of Chapter II is concerned with the situative conditions resulting from the abrupt omission of the relationship to the libretto, whereby the focus is displaced outside the textual frame of reference.

Chapter III briefly highlights the scope of three additional text-related parameters of the music in conjunction with their aesthetic issues: the specified titles of the works, the delineated expressive nuances, as well as the descriptive commentaries and textual depictions found in the score. Furthermore, the chapter outlines the consequences of two-dimensional theatricality and meta-theatricality.

In conclusion, the commentary argues that the compositional procedure adopts literary references for the benefit of creating self-generated concepts. In other words, constituted within a plethora of musical and extra-musical elements, texts function as energetic catalytic stimuli; they become the key mechanism to enhance interactive system performance amidst the music's structural-strategic and conceptual framework.

Table of Contents

I	**The Concept of Polymediality**	**9**
1.1	The Work-Immanent Compositional Dimension	9
1.2	The Vehicles Cycle	21
1.3	The Dimension of Staging	21
1.4	Quality versus Quantity	21
II	**Literary Sources as an Inherent Polymedial Element of Music**	**23**
2.1	The Implementation of Textual Elements and Vocality in Instrumental Works with Special Reference to the Orchestral Composition *Akanthai*	23
2.1.1	Historical Retrospective	23
2.1.2	Multiple Approaches of the Employment of Literary Sources in Instrumental Compositions	25
2.1.3	Comparative Motives	32
2.1.4	*Akanthai* and *The 9th of July 1821*	39
2.1.5	The Synergetic Interaction within *Akanthai*'s Heterogeneous Repertoire	40
2.1.6	The Varying Conditions of Integration and Individualization	53
2.1.7	The Polydimensional Articulation of Homogeneity	54
2.1.8	Conclusion	65
2.2	The Situative Conditions Resulting from the Abrupt Omission of the Relationship to the Literary Source on the Basis of Exemplary Excerpts from the Opera *Die Jagd*	67
III	**The Original Text-Related Parameters and the Consequences of Theatricality of the Music in *Akanthai* and *Die Jagd***	**85**

Appendix I: Polymediality, Percussivity, and Hybridity	91
Appendix II: References	99

CHAPTER I

The Concept of Polymediality

My work encompasses compositions in diverse genres and settings for opera and the concert hall, including multimedia and large-scale projects for cultural events. The central concept of this work is based on a qualitative polymediality that comprises two dimensions: the work-immanent compositional dimension and polymediality in the process of staging. In the first dimension, unconventional musical materials and music-extraneous media elements become integral components of the composition. In the second dimension, the composition interacts with other art forms and media.

1.1 The Work-Immanent Compositional Dimension

On the plane of composition, polymediality involves the factor of space – indoor and outdoor – in the musical and dramaturgical concept. The technical characteristics of the performance space are considered during the compositional phase and influence the construction of the work. In this context, as for the acoustic irradiation of the open-air square in *Autosymphonic* and the two-floor car showroom in the opera *Die Jagd*, a complex spatial system has been exclusively conceived in order to enable a surrounding effect, thus generating an amphitheatre of acoustical events. Thanks to the spatial conception, the placement of musicians (Diagram 1), and the 360-degree audio rendering, the sounds are retained in three-dimensional form throughout and a kind of sound holography emerges.

For the instrumental piece *En Plo*, an electrically operated scenographic draft, occuping both the stage and the audience area, participates in the acoustical, theatrical, physical, and thematic environment of the work. The score prescribes a devise for vibrating the audience seating during the collisions, two wind machines with powerful airflow situated at the back of the concert hall directed towards the audience, a ship's propeller, a capstan with anchor and steel chain. In *Strophes*, the extraordinary architectonic features of the Volkswagen Transparent Factory in Dresden influenced the production of sounds. To demonstrate an example, the trumpet's part exploits the plant's huge glass tower and glass elevator, either as reverberation effect transducer, damper, or pitch shifter. Such conceptions, however, are often unique and not repeatable, because they are designed in advance for a certain space.

Diagram 1: *Autosymphonic* – Open-air multimedia symphony (2010–11), 360-degree positioning of musical groups

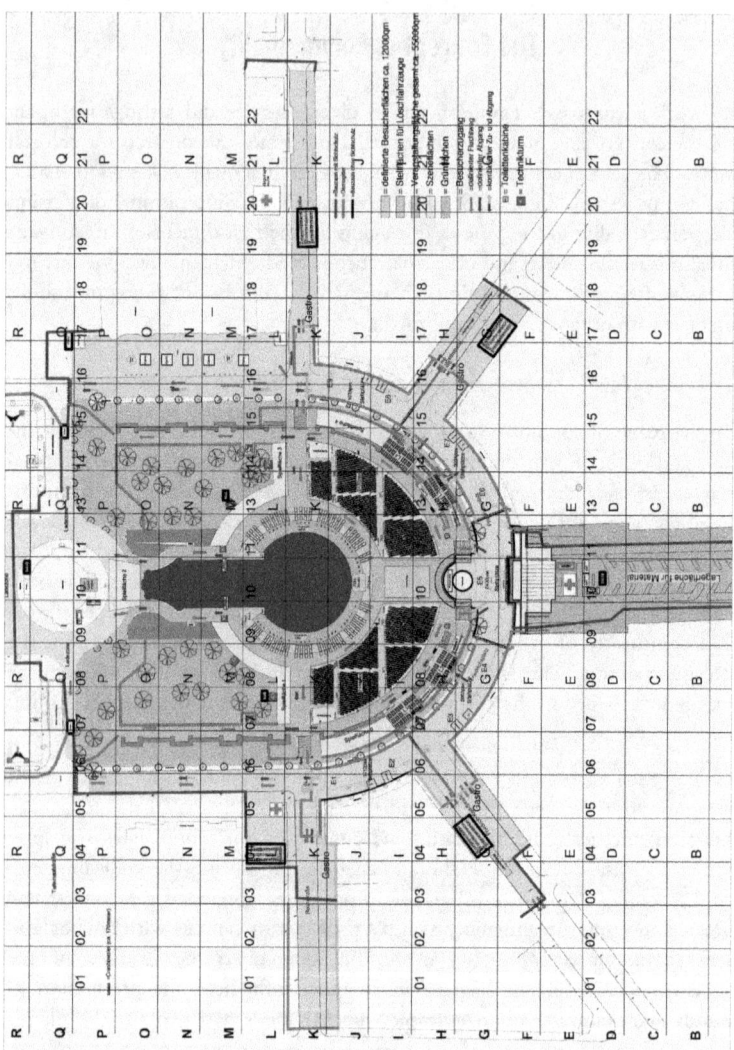

13 stage areas: 1. Main stage for symphony orchestra, choir and children's choir; 2.–5. Two smaller stages on the left and right sides of the main stage respectively for the percussion octet; 6.–7. Two smaller stages above water, opposite the main stage, for the singers and rappers of Söhne Mannheims; 8. Autoquartet ("Form Follows Function"); 9. Car orchestra I ("Genesis"); 10. Car orchestra II ("The Promise"); 11. Car orchestra III ("Virtual Reality"); 12. Car orchestra IV ("Finale"); 13. Car orchestra V consisting of trucks and busses

Additionally, the music incorporates extraneous musical elements,[1] electronic media and electroacoustic sounds, literary texts, theatrical and visual components. Through the exploitation of acoustic sources such as the automobile and machine parts in *Die Jagd*, *Strophes*, and *Autosymponic*, the possibilities of sound creation and playing techniques are extended. The prospects in machinery are particularly unique: I systematically investigate this potential, which permits heterogeneous sound mixtures of a hybrid of diverse automobile sounds and a polyphonic setting of the automobiles with instruments and voices.

A new context materializes from this atypical approach to traditional ensemble formations, and atypical ensemble formations are given traditional musical parameters:

i. In the case of *Staubzucker*, the guitar quartet is treated as a quasi-percussion group (Example 1b). The underlying idea is to downplay traditional guitar playing, and transfer a selection of sounds that are commonly produced on percussion instruments to the guitar (Example 1a). For example: (a) snare drum via crossed strings, (b) wood blocks via hitting/tapping the sidewalls of the body with knuckles, fingertips, fingernails, and open hand, (c) temple blocks played by the thumb of the left hand pulling the string extremely high, from the fingerboard away, and plucking, either with the edge of a bottleneck or with the flesh of the right hand thumb and left hand middle finger, on the string's left and right side, respectively, (d) conga via hitting the back of the instrument with the fist (inducing the resonation of the low E string), (e) whistle via the little finger's nail running along the string, (f) pop-gun effect via Bartók pizzicato on muted string.

ii. In Scene II of *Die Jagd*, "Nacht, Damals (A),"[2] the lights of the six cars are rhythmically composed. This episode is described in the score as "LICHTMUSIK (Lichtrhythmus),"[3] b. 59–74 (Example 2).

iii. The instrumentalists in *Akanthai* perform chanted elements that are textually assigned with expressive nuances.

---

[1] Unconventional instruments, non-European and folk instruments, speaking and shouting choruses.

[2] Night, Then (A).

[3] Light's Music (Light's Rhythm).

Example 1a: *Staubzucker* for guitar quartet (2007), list of instrumental and vocal sounds, score's remarks, pp. 2–3

A. **Percussion Sounds** (marked with "•")
   The transfer of distinctive sounds normally produced on percussion instruments is applied on the guitar – the guitar as a percussive apparatus:

   1. Snare drum (SD): crossed strings with L.H.
   2. Wood blocks (WB): on the sidewalls of the soundboard of the guitar (e.g. with knuckles, fingertips, fingernails, open hand)
   3. Temple blocks (TB): the thumb of the left hand pulling the string extremely high, from the fingerboard away, and plucking, either with the edge of a bottleneck or with the flesh of the right hand's thumb and left hand's middle finger, on the string's left (L) and right side (R), respectively
   4. Tom-tom (TT): on bridge (if not otherwise indicated)
   5. Bongo (B): on front (Bf) or back (Bb) surface of body
   6. Conga (C): hit with fist (right side) the back of the instrument inducing the resonation of the low E string
   7. Bass drum (BD): tambora (in front of bridge)
   8. Marimba (M): pizzicato; with R.H. thumb (flesh)
   9. Pop-gun effect (PG): Bartók pizz. explosively on the muted string (without definite pitch)
   10. Suspended Cymbal (crash) (CC): Bartók pizz. explosively at indicated position (with definite pitch)
   11. Suspended Cymbal (bowed) (CB): play the strings with a bow, near the bridge
   12. Bell (Be): clothespin on string
   13. Gong (G): harmonic on concrete pitch
   14. Wind chimes (bamboo like) (WC): harmonics on one position (e.g. XII) over strings with continuous arpeggiando
   15. Guiro (G): fast arpeggio over harmonics on highest position (e.g. XIX)
   16. Flexitone (F): with L.H. pressed first string over sound hole (approx. 12 cm. from bridge); rapid finger tremolo with R.H.
   17. Ratchet (R): either L.H. mutes all strings over sound hole; R.H.: continuous hard rasgueado, flamenco-like, over six strings (e.g. b. 35), or, with R.H. i-m finger tremolo and L.H. harmonic touch on given string and fret (e.g. b. 1)
   18. Whistle (W): little finger's nail run along the string
   19. Paper tearing (PT): scratching sound (+ glissando) with nail/s (thumb) along the low E string

20. Vibraslap (VS): long object (e.g. pencil) between (middle string) the three lower or three higher strings (centre of fret) – produces a 'bouncing' sound effect
21. Maracas (Ma): quick tremolo-rasgueado on two strings (interval: minor second)
22. Frame drum (wiping) (FD): with nails' surface or fingertips (flesh) rubbing a paper surface that is fixed (prepared) on the upper side part of the instrument (i) or with open hand rubbing the strings (ii)
23. Hi-hat (HH): hit on strings (thumb, palm; closed/open hand) over sound hole

B. **Voice** (indicated with a mouth sign, marked with "x"):

1. Bilabial snap (bs)
2. Tongue click (tc)
3. Breath (b); exhale (▶), inhale (◀)
4. Creaking voice (cv)
5. High lips tremolo with voice produced by the index, or high lips tremolo only with voice (lt)
6. Amerindian voice/scream (with or without hand) (iv); with tongue-tremolo
7. Whistle (with fingers) (w)

Example 1b: *Staubzucker*, b. 13–23

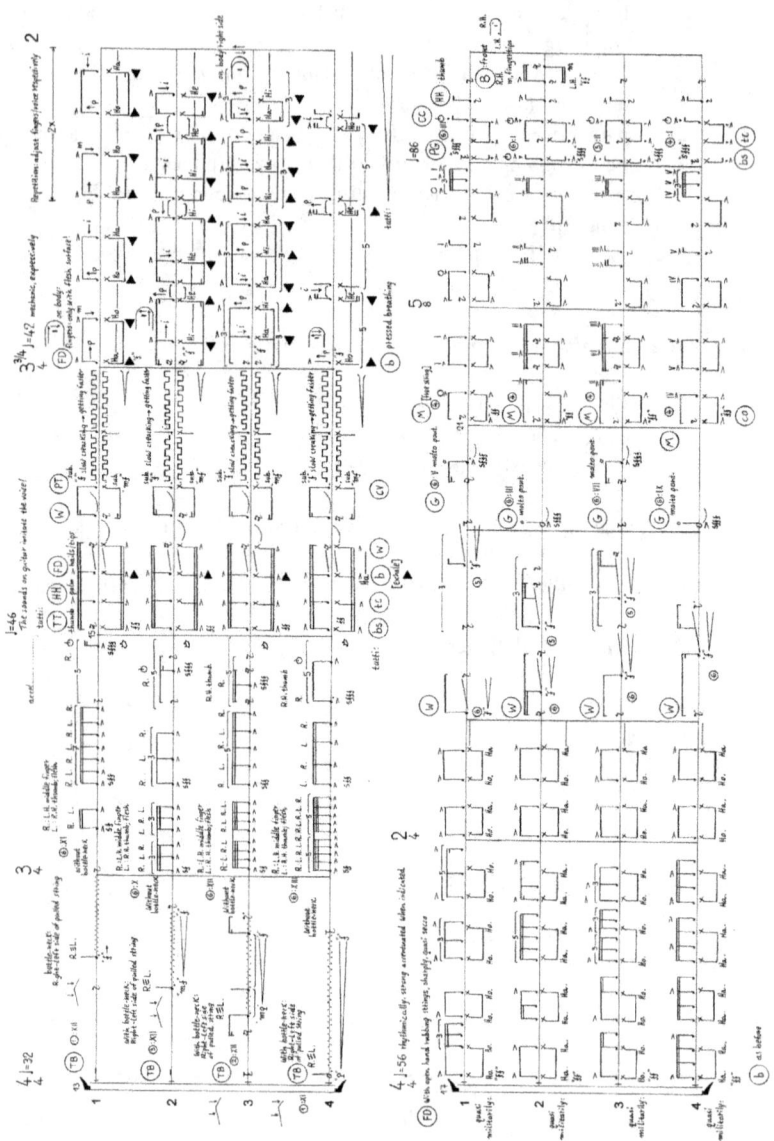

Example 2: *Die Jagd* – Opera for nature and cars (2008), Scene II, "Nacht, Damals (A)," "LICHTMUSIK (Lichtrhythmus)," b. 59–74

The following analysis of the Lichtmusik topos in *Die Jagd* aims to delineate the process of construction employing polymedial material in the music.

Looking for background information, the tempo marking MM=40 is ascribed to the preformatted electronic sounds that spatially surround the car sextet. The optical material exploited from the automobiles encloses the low (NL) and high-beam headlamp (GL), the brake lamp (BL), and the directional indicators (▲). Hence, polyphonic structures are designed from the perspective of a purely visual perception. The definitive notational parameters of music are nevertheless depicted here in the traditional fashion. Scoring unconventional material with conventional notational practice is not a paradox; it achieves performance practicality and effectiveness.

The musicians performing the car lights sit in the drivers' seats and play the lights in a manner similar to a drum kit: low and high beam headlamps are controlled with the hands, the brake lamp by the foot. GL resembles the bass drum, and this is correspondingly written as the lowest note on the staff.

Example 3 summarizes the fundamental rhythmic motifs on which Lichtmusik is built.

Example 3: *Die Jagd*, Scene II, "Nacht, Damals (A)," fundamental rhythmic motifs of "LICHTMUSIK (Lichtrhythmus)"

The lights episode consists of a series of micro-time-phrases. Three rhythmic modules construct the first phrase, bars 59–61, each sliding from one voice to the next. Automobile 6 (Ford Mustang) performs a tenuto crotchet (NL), followed by a staccatissimo semiquaver (GL). Auto 5 (Ford Focus ST) acts in counterpoint to the staccatissimo semiquaver of Auto 6. The length of the tenuto note of each of the subsequent two rhythmic modules is a semiquaver less than its precedent: crotchet → quaver and semiquaver → quaver. The phrase crescendos at the tutti semiquaver of the high beam headlamps. At bar 62, a regular repetition of the high beam headlamp, on triplets, occurs. Auto 1 (Aston Martin DB9 Volante) begins on the first note of the triplet, then Auto 2 (Jaguar SKR) on the second, Auto 3 (Land Rover Defender) on the third. In short, the aspect of mobility finds various applications in the music since sound (= light) is set in motion in a rotating state.

Bar 62 is directly related to the central phrase of the lights section, "LICHTTANZ," later in bars 66–70. Despite the fact that bar 62 does not appear side-by-side with the Lichttanz, it functions as a preamble for the dance. The generated graphic (Diagram 2) illustrates the manifestation of the staggered homophony of the triplets in bars 66–68. It distinctly depicts the same concept of regular movement passing through the voices by each note of the triplet, marked in orange, as in bar 62. Focussing on the overall structure, it emphasizes the irregular alternation between activity and rest, by which dramaturgy emerges.

In contextualizing the quotation in "LICHTTANZ" together with the time signature of 3/4, the compositional approach adopts traits of the waltz, but it attempts to subjectively interpret those traits by giving them a different semiotic form. As a consequence, the step sequence of the waltz of 1 (long) – 2 (short) – 3 (short), is reflected in the triplet figuration, the only rhythmic element in Lichtmusik's first three bars.

Diagram 2: *Die Jagd*, Scene II, "Nacht, Damals (A)," "LICHTTANZ," b. 66–68, rhythmic structural cascade in triplets

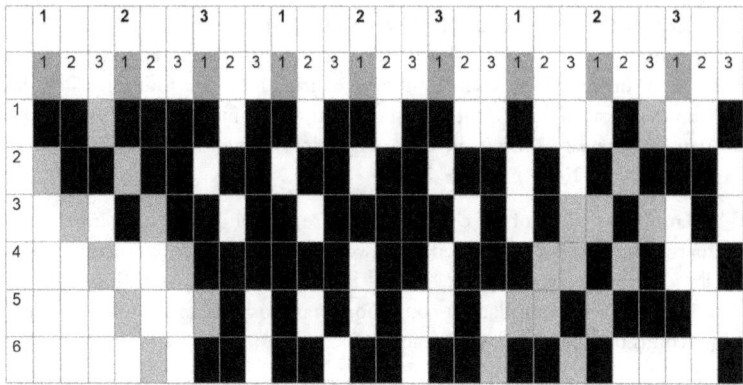

There is always a degree of coherence between heterogeneous segments. Interrelationships are established on a technical and conceptual plane through the deployment of montage techniques: the short cello-piano phrase, which appeared earlier in bars 39–41, precedes the lights section. Similar to the Lichttanz passage (b. 62, 66–70), the progression is split up. What this implies is that a precomposed segment is fractured and its parts are located separately within the score. The cello-piano phrase softly advances throughout in rhythmical unison, on semiquavers, resembling a repeated two-step movement (b. 56–58, Example 4). Thus, the cello-piano phrase and the waltz gesture of the car lights provide evidence of the uniform approach envisioned amid the opera's widely divergent elements.

In respect of this context, the actress Isabel performs a complex rhythmicized narration during both parts (b. 39–41 and 56–58). Her articulated line[4] "Dennoch hatte ich bald ein Gefühl, ein Misstrauen,"[5] initializes the Lichtmusik section, a portrayal of the bizarre and imaginary forest in the music ("Wald-Erinnerung III"[6]). The car ensemble represents a herd of forest creatures; the car lights, the eyes of these creatures in the darkness.

Isabel's words "Waren meine Vorahnungen falsch? Sollte es einen Zustand danach geben?"[7] signal the closing of Lichtmusik. Immediately after, the boy

---

[4] Here and in the following, English translations or any original non-English texts will be provided in the footnotes.

[5] However, soon I had a suspicious feeling.

[6] Third forest recollection.

[7] Were my forebodings misplaced? What could possibly happen next?

soprano Benni sings a three-bar melody on the word "Reset" repeated polyphonically by the two instrumental groups. The pitch configuration applied is processed by the same method as the cello-piano's harmonic texture. It is based on two minor thirds, E – G and F – A♭, at first sung linearly by the boy soprano and subsequently expanded in octave formations over four ranges by the instruments (Example 6), within a polyrhythmic context that resembles the structure of the car horns at the opera's culmination point in Scene XIV, "Isas Jagd," b. 310–311 (see Example 27).

The harmonic texture of the cello-piano phrase is built on two perfect fourths.[8] A quartal chord ensues, extended over two and a half octaves, consisting of the pitches, from lowest to highest, of C – F♯ – C♯ – F – C – F♯ (Example 5). The interval succession places a continuous transposition and inversion of minor seconds over three octaves (Example 7).

Example 4: *Die Jagd*, Scene II, "Nacht, Damals (A)," b. 56–58, cello-piano sequence

Example 5: Harmonic development of the cello-piano sequence

Example 6: b. 80–86¹, Harmonic constitution & Example 7: Cello-piano's interval variations

---

[8] C – F, C♯ – F♯.

1.2 The Vehicles Cycle

Die Jagd and *Autosymphonic* are part of a larger cycle of works in which different vehicle types are employed as musical instruments. Bicycles played in *Der Wegweiser*,[9] Harley-Davidson motorcycles in *Tempus Tantum Nostrum Est*,[10] aviation elements in *Die Reise des G. Mastorna*,[11] and ship components in *En Plo*[12] are given sound-producing roles. For the first time, the automobile, as a pivotal motive and artistic medium, was integrated into *Strophes* in 2003.

1.3 The Dimension of Staging

Within the framework of staging, the music or, more precisely, the holistic nature of musical synthesis, interacts dynamically with other art forms and media, as in the case of *Die Jagd* and *Autosymphonic*.

The lineaments of holistic musical synthesis are systemic, synthetic, and summative. Included is the intellectual and intuitive grasp of the ideas behind the music, since it often attempts to render an extra-musical narrative, as well as all music-extraneous media elements that are integral components of the score. The significance of the smallest segments that might be considered units can only be understood in terms of their contribution to the significance of the whole. The latter is therefore epistemologically prior.

Holistic polymediality is not just the sum of the music and its staging, but also the compositional effect of the summative image of the music being staged.

1.4 Quality versus Quantity

The creative process embeds an all-encompassing dramaturgy and aesthetic consistency. The quantity of media is less important than the sense-establishing ratio of the music in its interaction with other media and arts. I define my work on the basis of a synergistic (active and mutually stimulating) interaction between the music and the employed agencies. Although the media are entangled with one another, each retains its individuality.

The utilization of vehicles has a strong contextual reference: the themes of wanderlust, discovery, and adventure are central inspirational motives that incite the creation of associated sound structures. In *Autosymphonic*, for example, the history of the automobile, based on Carl Benz's autobiography, is mir-

---

[9] Premiered at the Berlin Philharmonic, 2005.

[10] Premiered at the Salzburg Biennial, 2005.

[11] Premiered at the Salzburg Airport, 2006.

[12] Premiered at the Akademie der Künste Berlin, 2007.

rored in an idiosyncratic way in the music. Methodologically observed, the compositional procedure is construed as a permanent change of perspectives, thus reflecting a multifaceted movement.

CHAPTER II

Literary Sources as an Inherent Polymedial Element of Music

2.1 The Implementation of Textual Elements and Vocality in Instrumental Works with Special Reference to the Orchestral Composition *Akanthai*

The instrumental works *Akanthai* for large orchestra, *Staubzucker* for guitar quartet, and *Thalatta, Thalatta!* for mandolin and ensemble are demonstrably influenced by extra-musical references. The overall musical outcome is, however, predominantly unaffected by this. Only certain pre-determined momentary contours might suggest direct programmatic evidence. In this case, the extra-musical narrative is rendered through the application of vocally focused passages. It is worth remarking that even in the opera *Die Jagd* which embraces vocal soloists, singing and speaking choirs, instrumental groups are also used in a vocal fashion.

When a piece includes vocal elements, the foremost question that arises concerns the existence of a textual source. This may challenge the substance, contextualization, and modus operandi manifested within its musical structures. Therefore, in order to exemplify how the methodological perspective deals with texts, I will refer to *Akanthai*. Subsequent to a brief musical-historical retrospective, there will be an outline of multiple approaches to literary sources as they occur in some of my other instrumental compositions. This is in addition to a comparative discourse that testifies to the impact of Greek chorus, Balinese kecak, and Cypriot folk music on a series of distinctive parts from *Akanthai*. The commentary aims at elaborating the hypothesis that musical and non-musical elements, such as literary sources, are mustered with coherent principles. At the same time it is to question and investigate the correlations in the repertoire of the composition out of exemplary score-cuts.

Throughout the commentary, I make use of the word repertoire separately from its conventional linguistic usage. The unique context encompasses the entirety of composed musical materials plus all built-in non-musical elements.

2.1.1 Historical Retrospective

In the history of twentieth- and early twenty-first-century music, there is frequently the requirement for instrumentalists to act vocally. A typical example is *Antiphonen* for viola and twenty-five instrumentalists by Bernd Alois Zimmermann (1961–62). In the fourth antiphon, instead of playing, the musicians have to speak an eight-lingual text montage: the *Apocalypse of John* in Greek,

Dante Alighieri's *Divine Comedy* in Italian, and James Joyce's *Ulysses* in English.[13] The multifariousness of the employed languages evokes a universalistic superelevation that elicits the question, whether therein lay the decisive selection criterion for those texts. Zimmermann maintained the argument that the chosen texts encompass semantic and phonetic functions.[14] The structurally precise organization of the composition models the sound in its antiphonal, pluralistic ramifications, and polymorphism: sound colour occurs as a result of the musical material's strict concentration with vocal inserts as orchestral colours. Understanding the words from the instrumentalist-speaker's interpretation is not of primary, but secondary importance. The result of the vocal insertions is analogous to the instrumental sound colouration.

It is no coincidence that the transition of the music in the language appears at the moment of the soloist's cadence. This becomes the convergence point where the integration of external elements follows. Zimmermann perceived the use of linguistic material as a natural tangent of the verbal emanating from the non-verbal, an escalation of the absolute music in the language comparable to Ludwig van Beethoven's Symphony No. 9 where Friedrich Schiller's words are first sung during the final movement by four vocal soloists and a chorus.

A further example is Mauricio Kagel's *Anagrama* for soloists, speaking chorus, and chamber ensemble (1957–58), which utilizes a spoken phase for the instrumentalists, albeit very short. The key difference between Kagel and Zimmermann is that Kagel incorporated the theatrical aspect of performance itself – the instrumentalists' vocal actions – as a new compositional parameter in a traditionally non-theatrical genre. In contrast, Zimmermann concerns himself more with the perspectives of suggestion and gesture than of actual action.

It seems conceivable that the vocal insertions of the instrumentalists construe a continuation of the propensity coined by Felix Mendelssohn's *Songs without Words*; namely, letting texts resonate in flux between the physical and the imaginary.[15] On a related note, the symphonic poems of Franz Liszt and the tone poems of Richard Strauss imply an orchestral piece in free form whose music is evoked by a poetic or narrative text.

---

[13] Additionally excerpts from the books of Job and Ecclesiastes, Dostoyevsky's *The Brothers Karamazov*, Camus's *Caligula*, and Novalis's *Hymn to the Night*, were used.

[14] For example, the acoustic and expressive properties inherent in the original language.

[15] Compare Charles-Valentin Alkan's *Chants* and Edvard Grieg's *Lyric Pieces*.

2.1.2 Multiple Approaches of the Employment of Literary Sources in Instrumental Compositions

C Story for tenor, mixed western and non-western instruments, 2006, (Example 8) is inspired by the short poem *Cyprus History* by Costas Montis:

> Endless years of slavery – their slap and their kick.
> We stick there: Olive trees and carob trees on top of their rock.[16]

The tutti emergent gestalts appear strongly but ephemerally from within the composition. These are a musical gesture corresponding to the words "slap" and "kick." Such examples of germane sound impulses embrace the snare drum rimshot, the marimba dead stroke, the Bartók pizzicato (slapping) and martellato (hammered) of the strings, the pan flute's slap, the beating on a leather case with the birch, and the percussively voiced "Ha" through the megaphone. The inserted vocal particles – either performed by the tenor or the entire instrumental ensemble – do not deliver any textual ingredients of the poem. Alternatively, sonically contrived reproductions of the inherent dynamism of the words – through non-semantic phonetic expressions and instrumental sounds – expose Montis's central message of persistent resistance.

The employment of textual elements in *Thalatta, Thalatta!* for mandolin and ensemble (2007) (Example 9) is somewhat different. Impulsive words, people's names, and numbers are vocally interjected as purely acoustical expressions. They do not emanate from any concrete external reference; they are devised after a relocation of events initially depicted in Xenophon's literary and historic narration *Anabasis*. Additionally, the composition absorbs the antithetical words "anabasis" (ascent) and "katabasis" (descent), and transfers them to a plethora of sound events. Within bars 1–6, (a) the glissando directions, (b) the groups of ascending and descending tones and microtones, (c) the arpeggio scales, (d) the bow transition from bridge to fingerboard, and vice versa, (e) the expeditious register change from extremely high to extremely low (piano et al.), (f) the air flutter-tonguing downwards of the bass clarinet, and (g) the elastically springing element of the mandolin and violoncello yield a subjective acoustical aura of the related nouns.

---

[16] Χρόνια, σκλαβκιὲς ἀτέλειωτες—τὸμ πάτσον τζαὶ τὸγ κλῶτσον τους. / Ἐμεῖς τζαμαί: Ἐλιὲς τζαὶ τερατσιὲς πάνω στὸρ ρότσον τους.

Example 8: *C Story* for tenor, mixed western and non-western instruments (2006), b. 41–45

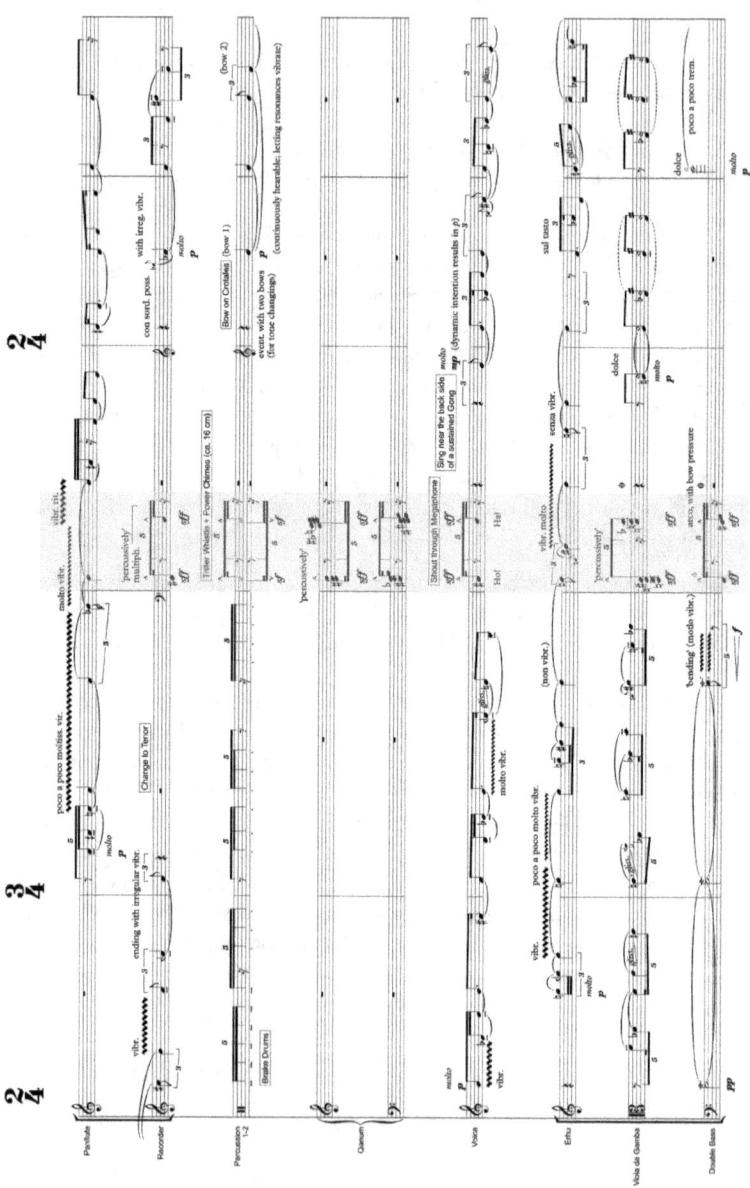

Example 9: *Thalatta, Thalatta!* for mandolin and ensemble (2007), b. 1–6

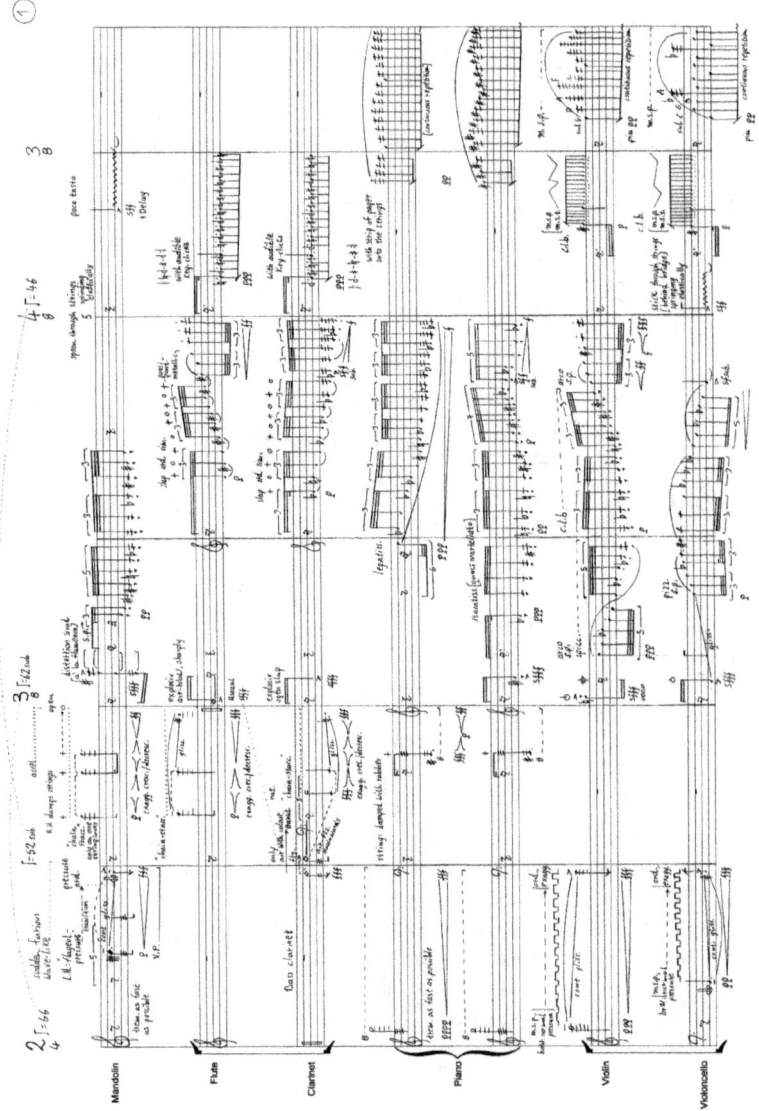

Der Wegweiser for sinfonietta (2005) is a sequel to the homonymous Schubert song from the cycle *Winterreise* (Example 10).[17] The literary backdrop draws upon the poem cycle by Wilhelm Müller set to music by Franz Schubert, and is additionally juxtaposed with Constantine Cavafy's poem *Ithaca*. The theme of the voyage evokes the inclusion of journey-associated sound apparatuses, like the bicycle wheels and the old typewriter, the musician's positioning scheme on stage (Diagram 3), and the involvement of neutral spoken elements derived from the traffic signs, such as "Halt!" and "Einbahnstrasse!," and supplemented by the audience's motivating shouts that occur at a sporting event, such as "Los!" and "Avanti!"[18]

Diagram 3: *Der Wegweiser*, zig-zag positioning, score's remarks, p. 4

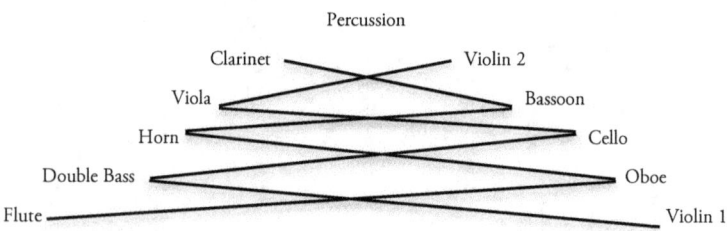

Totes Kleid[19] for recorders and sewing machine (2005) owes its threnodic-hinted character, expressed via the diverse vibrato types and the partial colouring of the vibrato by means of unison vocalizations direct in the instrument, the utilization of the sewing machine, and the playing method of two simultaneous soprano recorders in the reflection of a Cypriot folk song/text, entitled *Four and Four*.[20] Turning to *Cicadas* for amplified piano (2005) (Ex. 11), the initial antecedent is an extract from the radio drama of same name by Ingeborg Bachmann (Ex. 12, Text 1). During the composition's preparation, a second text of a radically divergent form from Bachman's was created (Text 2). Subsequently, a kind of cryptographic text message develops (Text 2, bold). The alphabet letters of the latter are liberally substituted with a series of notes. Each letter corresponds to a specific pitch, thus a piano key. The piano is envisioned as a typewriter, on which the cryptographic text is documented. All typewriter sound effects are reproduced analogously with extended piano techniques.

---

[17] The Fingerpost.
[18] Stop!, One-way street!, Go!, Ahead!
[19] Dead Dress.
[20] Τέσσερα τζιαι Τέσσερα.

Example 10: *Der Wegweiser* for sinfonietta (2005), b. 40–42

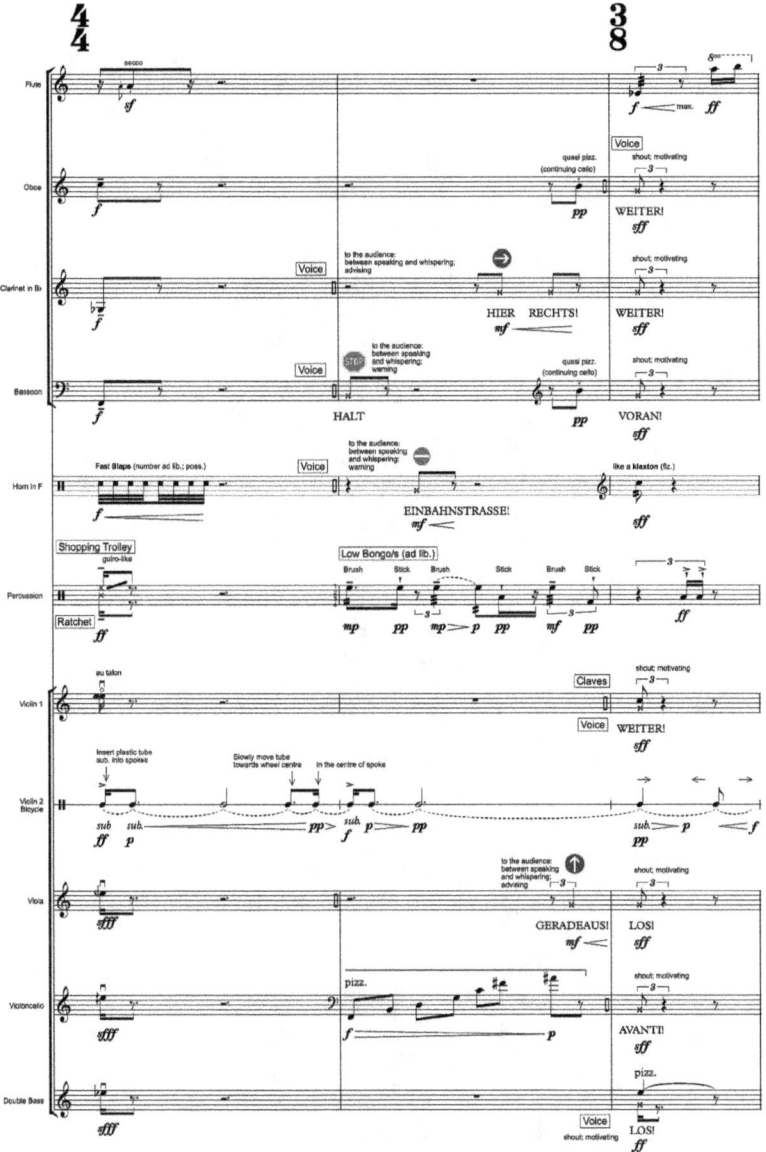

Example 11: *Cicadas* for amplified piano (2005), b. 8–10

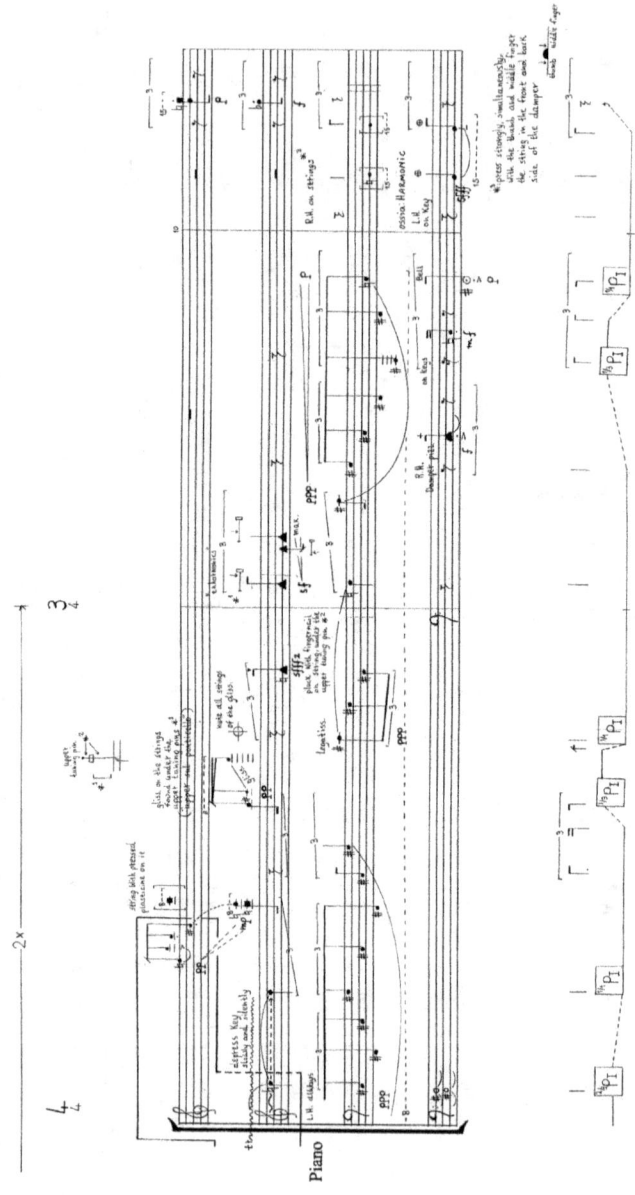

Example 12: *Cicadas*, textual transformation

Text 1: *Die Zikaden* by Ingeborg Bachmann (1954)

Denn die Zikaden waren einmal Menschen.
Sie hörten auf zu essen,
zu trinken und zu lieben,
um immerfort singen zu können.

Auf der Flucht in den Gesang
wurden sie dürrer und kleiner,
und nun singen sie,
an ihre Sehnsucht verloren – verzaubert,
aber auch verdammt,
weil ihre Stimmen unmenschlich geworden sind.[21]

Text 2: *Zikaden* by Marios Joannou Elia (2005)

Die Menschen
werden zu essen auf...hören,
zu trinken, lieben auf...hören,
um immerfort singen zu können.

Auf der Flucht in den Gesang
werden sie dürrer und kleiner,
in einer Streichholzschachtel schlafen.
Zugleich werden sie singen,
an ihre Sehnsucht verloren – verzaubert,
dazu verurteilt,
weil ihre Stimmen unerträglich sein werden.

Das Wasser im Meer wird süß.
Es werden keine Märchen mehr an Kindern erzählt werden,
weil, eines Tages, die Menschen verwandeln sich in Zikaden!

Jetzt sind sie im Reisekoffer.
Das ein oder andere Mal hören sie, entfernt, das Sin...gen.

Und wenn sie keinen Mund haben werden?
Sparren sie das Salz, die Zik-Adern![22]

---

[21] Once upon a time the cicadas were human beings. / They stopped eating, / drinking and loving / in order to be able to sing forever.
Upon their flight into song / they became thinner and smaller, / and now they sing / lost to their longing – enchanted / but also damned / because their voices have become inhuman.

[22] The human beings / will stop to eat ... listen, / will stop to drink, love ... listen / in order to be able to sing forever.

2.1.3 Comparative Motives

Between bars 102 and 106 in *Akanthai* fifty-five instrumentalists must perform the vibrant vocal passage "But ... when the aging poplar is cut down" (Example 13). This section, which flows in rhythmical unison, is not unintentional; it is linked to four verses of the epic poem *The 9th of July 1821* by Vasilis Michaelides, written in the Greek-Cypriot dialect in 1893:

> (...) but be warned that when the aging poplar is cut down
> all around it three hundred new sprouts shoot up.
> The ploughshare while ploughing the earth, thinks the earth is wasted,
> but it is itself that's always wasted and itself that's worn out.[23]

When the orchestral musicians act vocally, they embody a large choir. This metamorphosis or transmutation of the sound from instrumental to vocal is comparable to the chorus's function and its musical properties in ancient Greek theatre.

The fact that all performers of Greek drama were simultaneously trained as singers and dancers signifies a hybrid function. Choral lyrics were choreographed and sung in unison to melodically and rhythmically complex musical accompaniment. The chorus was a group of minor actors who could portray any character, and voice the hidden fears or secrets the protagonists could not express. Tragedy and comedy were born out of improvisational beginnings. According to Aristotle, tragedy developed from the dithyramb, a Dionysian hymn that was sung and danced in circular formations by a chorus of up to fifty men, boys, or maidens. Dance movements included rows with interweaving movements, acrobatic leaps, splits, processionals, as well as dances of victory, defeat, and madness.

The tight and sometimes obscure syntax of some choral songs, especially by Sophocles, provides evidence that their words must have been nearly always distinctly heard, for otherwise they would have been unintelligible to many.

Upon their flight into song / they will become thinner and smaller, / sleep in a matchbox. / At the same time they will sing, / lost to their longing – enchanted, / but sentenced, / because their voices will become unbearable.
The water in the sea will become sweet. / No more fairy tales will be told to children, / because, one day, human beings will transform themselves into cicadas.
Now they are inside the luggage. / One or the other time, they listen, away, the singing.
And if they will have no mouth? / They save the salt, the capricious cicadas!

[23] (...) αμμά ξέρε πως υλαντρον όντας κοπεί καβάτζιν / τριγύρου του πετάσσουνται τρακόσια παραπούλια. / Το 'νιν αντάν να τρώ' την γην, τρώει την γην θαρκέται, / μα πάντα τζιείνον τρώεται τζιαι τζιείνον καταλυέται.

For this reason, and as the Greek amphitheatres were outsized, the chorus's actions had to be exaggerated and their voices clearly projected in order to be acoustically and visually perceivable to everyone. Techniques commensurate with synchronization, echo, ripple, and physical theatre attained the latter.

Example 13: *Akanthai*, version for large orchestra (2009), b. 102–107

It is remarkable that characteristics of the ancient Greek chorus are traceable in the east, and, more precisely, in the chorus of the Balinese music drama called kecak. Although the modern form of kecak originates in the 1930s, the present mode is a result of a cross-cultural interaction between its roots in the ancient Hindu epic *Ramayana* and Western influence.[24] Kecak is nicknamed monkey chant, because the percussive chanting that accompanies the performance sounds like the chattering of monkeys. Moreover, the sound can be regarded as a vocal imitation of the gamelan orchestra. Hence, the voice is processed instrumentally. In other words, the chant, that is, the speaking choir, is to be heard as an analogue to instrumental music.

Originally, kecak was a trance-inducing exorcism dance accompanied by male chorus. A large chorus of more than a hundred bare-chested young men sat close together in a concentric circle and vocalized a complex rhythmic chant. With changing speed and volume, they called "cak-cak-cak" or "kecak kecak cak-a-cak." Such vocal expressions are reminiscent of the Dada movement, which had its heyday in the late 1910s and early 1920s, and the Dadaistic poems with expressive meaningless combination of sounds. Kecak includes choreographic elements in a similar manner to the Greek chorus. The chanters accompany their human orchestra with group movements, sometimes quickly fluttering their fingers with outstretched arms, sometimes moving their shoulders back and forth, or with isolated and staccato gestures as they turn their heads from side to side together with hands on waists. Body percussion, like hand clapping, is additionally incorporated into the performance.

The vocal music of kecak is a mixture of regular and irregular rhythmical patterns. The regular vocal forms use even beat rhythms based on short repeated patterns or ostinati. The irregular vocal forms, typically sung monophonic, are characterized by the practice of uneven beats in the singing, along with sounds that imitate expressive voices and nature. A chorus leader, comparable to Greek coryphaeus, coordinates the complex and multilayered incantation alongside the basic chanters. He gives signals by hand clapping, calling, and shouting.

The integration of vocal inserts within *Akanthai* alludes to the chorus's characteristic features of ancient Greek drama and Balinese kecak in several respects. For a paradigmatic example of practical applications of the contemplation, refer to the passage between bar 88 and bar 92 (see Sections 2.1.5. and 2.1.7., Example 17). At this singular juncture, the underlying word "Kyprianos" is

---

[24] For the German film making of *Insel der Dämonen* by Victor Baron von Plessen, Friedrich Dalsheim and Walter Spies (1933), kecak's traditional forms were liberally remodelled.

not to be found in Michaelides's verses. Although it is not the instrumentalists' first vocal entry, it is the first noticeable semantic text element in the score.

In bar 71, the appearance of vocality in chronological order begins in an acoustically shaded manner, almost unnoticed. Here, the vocality's function is to serve merely as spoken impulse for playing the mouth organ. Uninterrupted until bar 78, the vocal performance consists of wordless chant, vocalized with sounds such as rapid reiteration between "tu" and "ku", "tu" with vibrato, "tr(u)" by rolling "r" with the mouth modelled in a u-shape, or "tu-ku tu-ku" in variable, approximated speaking pitch levels. The group of syllables consisting of a vowel and consonants are executed in a percussive, mechanic-like, and repetitive fashion that resembles kecak's chanting.

Similar sounds are also present in the ancient comedies, like in the plays *The Frogs*, *The Birds*, and *The Wasps* of Aristophanes. In *The Frogs*, for example, the refrain of frog chorus begins with "Brekekekex koax koax," intending to imitate the croaking of frogs. Hence, the sounds of the frog chorus, likewise of kecak, imitate or suggest the source of the sound that they describe. In *Akanthai* nonetheless, "tu-ku-tu-ku" has a purely auditory quality.

Equivalent syllabic formations construct the textual material of the hunting choir, Jagdchor, the juvenile vocal ensemble in *Die Jagd*'s Scene IV, "Geräusche."[25] Contiguous to "tu-ku," all its vowel variations, ta-ka, to-ko, te-ke, ti-ki, constitute the lyrics of the percussive chant-like sequence in bars 59–62 (Example 14) and 67–72 (Example 22). The juvenile vocal ensemble incorporates woodland creatures; the scene being situated amidst the forest. As a result, these non-semantic combinations of sounds become allied with the hunting choir's peculiar physiognomy, in concert with its concealed onomatopoetic origin.

Referring back to *Akanthai*, the non-instrumental elements begin with hand clapping, bar 68, signalizing the beginning of the tu≡ku-passage in bar 71. The action takes place within a series of percussive timbres before the Bartók pizzicato, whip, and ratchet, and after a glass smashing noise of two bottles that are flung with full power against an iron plate. Hand clapping occurs anew in bar 110, setting a dynamic accent to the previously evolved fingertips tremolo on the corpus of the strings (Example 18). Paper bags burst explosively and tongue clicks follow as imitation variants of hand clapping, thus forming a transsegmental kinetic chain and an esemplastic image that emanates from a series of dissimilar sound sources.

The kaleidoscopic range of percussive timbre is integrated with a great variety of special sounds produced by the entire orchestra. Apart from instrumental

---

[25] Noises.

and vocalized material, *Akanthai* makes use of unconventional sound apparatuses, like corporal percussion, water surfaces, mouth organs and whistles, smashing bottles and vocal effects. Generally speaking, the inclusion of extraneous components in music is not uncommon; it is evidenced in Cypriot folk music. An additional introduction of sound producers that may not necessarily be musical instruments is employed in the Cypriot tradition of folk instrumentarium. Typical examples include whistles, conch shells, shepherd's bells, carnival rattles, and wooden or metal bars struck with a hammer. Moreover, the dance rhythms are accompanied by hand clapping, finger snapping, foot stomping, or with whistling and non-semantic, vocally expressed fillips. Time and rhythm is occasionally beaten out on cooking utensils.

From the perspective of contemporary music, such sound sources are comparable to the devices used by Mauricio Kagel. Since the 1960s, Kagel has particularly explored and expanded the concept of musical instruments. My research, however, is not simply aiming to achieve an alternative instrumentation and develop substitutional playing techniques; it intends to incorporate an extended instrumentarium in a mixture and juxtaposition with traditional materials, not neglecting the musician's fundamental technical skills, but constructing thereon. Accordingly, the repertoire employed presupposes an implication of heterogeneous elements.

Heterogeneity means that two objects may not share common properties. Their microstructures are different, thus instead of homogeneous notes, we speak of heterogeneous sound objects. Contextualizing the concept of a musical note just before Kagel's experiments, Pierre Schaeffer defined a short sound from any origin as *objet sonore*. The notion of sound object, as Curtis Roads says, generalizes the note concept in two ways:

> Certain sound objects may function as unique singularities. Entire pieces may be constructed from nothing but such singularities
>
> And
>
> It discards the notion of static, time-invariant properties in favour of time-varying properties (*Microsound*, p. 19).

In relation to *Akanthai*, a sound constituent, independently of its source, usually tends to accommodate its identity – without neglecting its diacritic character – into a homogeneous texture or mixture. The transition implies the model of imitative interaction, affected by the timbral property of the generating sound cell. The mimetic principal, a procedure derived from Aristotelian mimesis, is primarily an autonomous interpretation method that rests on source material (see Section 3.1.7.).

Example 14: *Die Jagd*, Scene IV, "Geräusche," b. 59–62

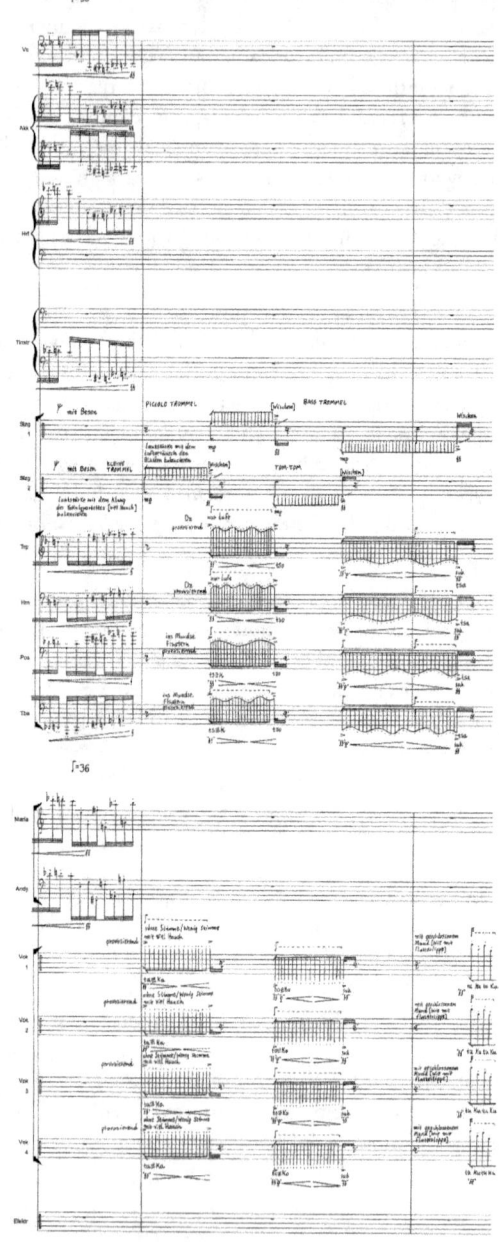

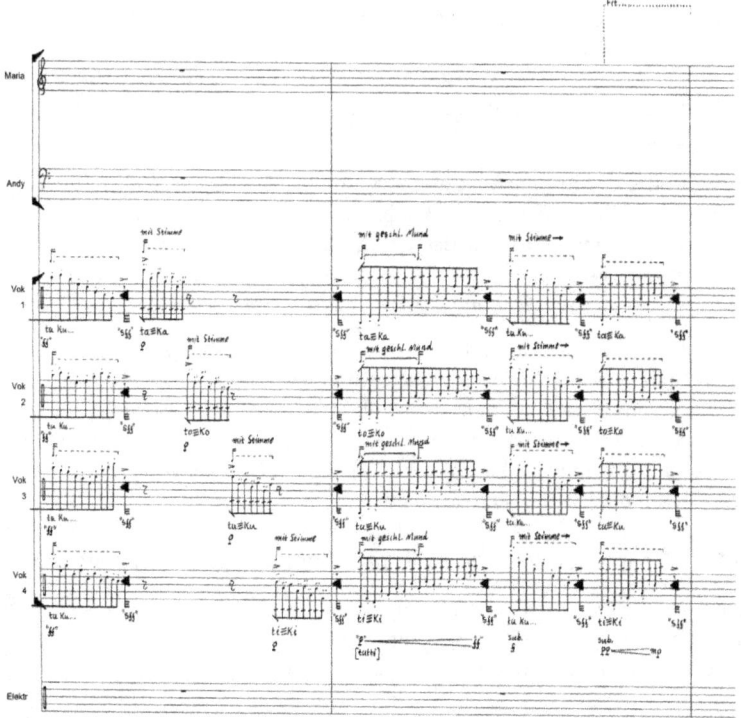

2.1.4 *Akanthai* and *The 9th of July 1821*

Akanthai integrates a pendulous, transient recitation of the four selected verses of *The 9th of July 1821* by Michaelides. Comparing the orchestra's attitude before, during, and after the text passages, the Michaelides's insertions possess a considerable measure of outbursts. A programmatic musical fabric results from the immense emotional and energetic potential that is contained in the dramatic narration: The 560 verses of the epic poem by Michaelides (here v. 183–186) describe the incidents surrounding the struggle for independence of the Hellenic population of the island of Cyprus that culminate in the arrest, conviction, and hanging of Archbishop Kyprianos on July 9, 1821.

Akanthai portrays the inconceivability of the act of the execution by way of the infused confusion of the text. The employed strategy articulates this dimension as an expressive component, like in bar 132 (Example 16): syllable/letter splitting; partially intensified verbal elements; individually as-fast-as-possible; and tutti dynamically exaggerated. Hence, the sound itself is subject to a dramatic manifestation.

Michaelides's poetry serves as a catalyst for augmenting the traditional comportment of the orchestra: for example, the vocal fragments enhance the orchestra by expanding its material. At the same time, the primary character of the orchestra as an instrumental ensemble remains intact: it is considerably intensified with colouristic and artificial semantic chant particles.

The stanza extracts epitomize the resistance of Archbishop Kyprianos against the Ottoman pasha Kucuk Mehmet, whose vigorous contradiction becomes immersed in the symbolism of the words. The sound in *Akanthai* is treated as an increase of text and its content-related idiosyncrasies. The compositional work with text implies that the text is concurrently materialistic and a reference point to the compositional process.

2.1.5 The Synergetic Interaction within *Akanthai*'s Heterogeneous Repertoire

Akanthai's work-immanent compositional polymediality pre-eminently implies transfer of information by the medium of literature to music. Literary and musical elements are inextricably interdependent and interwoven in the inner construction of the musical constellation, yet each element retains its individual identity.

Akanthai incorporates a heterogeneous repertoire, the components of which are not just structurally positioned via fusion or combination, but by way of contextualization, and from the resistance or antithesis that exists amongst them. The statement therefore entails:

i. That unconventional instrumental elements become the focus of attention and have a distinct existence from the orchestra's sound. This is evidenced by the rhythmical clapping of the hands, followed by the whip, in bars 68–69;

ii. That the orchestral sound maintains an equally intense degree of interaction with the vocal inserts, as illustrated by the gradual increase of the sequence's volume in bars 170–176 (Example 15);

iii. That sporadically vocal inserts attach more weightiness than instrumental sounds, like the speaking choir soloistic sequence in bars 132–134 (Example 16);

iv. That the polyphonic orchestral sound migrates to absolute vocal monophonic texture, and vice versa. In other words, the instrumental sound prolongs the chanting/vocality, and, depending on the interaction, the chanting/vocality continues the instrumental sound – as featured in the orchestral progression before (b. 124–131) and after (b. 135–138) the previous example;

v. That the text conserves an independent line within an orchestral polyphonic architecture, as exemplified by the five-bar fragment of "Ky – prrri, a – a – a – a – a, nos! nos! nos!" in bars 88–92 (Example 17);

vi. That the text, or fragments thereof, remain recognisable, not necessarily acoustically, but traceable in the score. The phonetics of the language, versus the actual content of the text, profits from the inherent autonomous musical intensities. In this instance, the words are as an entity or in part semantically unintelligible, as demonstrated in the preceding passage from "Kyprianos." Alternatively, the short selective phases of the distinct utterance of words provoke vocal emphasis and semantic transparency, as illustrated by the intense and repetitive consecution of the words "The share" at the composition's closing section (b. 170–177, Example 15);

vii. That vocal and instrumental lines are homogenously designed, as evidenced by the chant sequence "But… when the aging poplar is cut down" and the opposed strings, percussion 2, and piano phrase in rhythmical unison, bars 102-106 (Example 13). Here, the vocal emerges as instrumental; the instrumental suggestively transmutes into spontaneous vocality;

Example 15: *Akanthai*, b. 170–175

Example 16: *Akanthai*, b. 129–131

b. 132–134

b. 135–138

Example 17: *Akanthai*, Kypranos passage, b. 88–92

b. 93–101

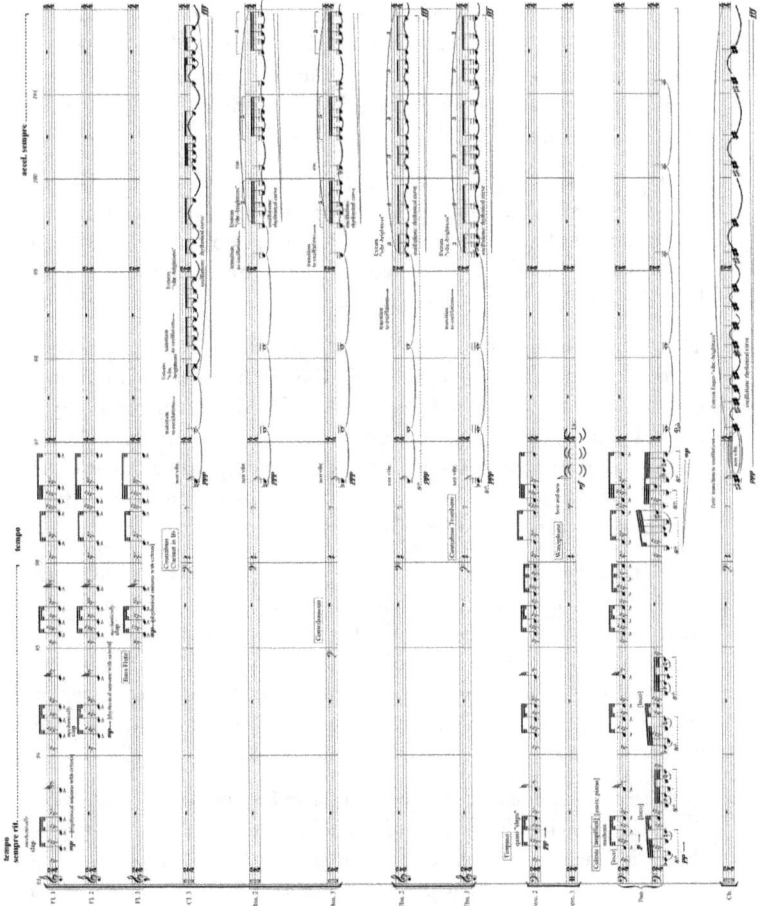

viii. That vocality assumes an instrumental quality and hence it behaves purely instrumentally, as in the series of alternating instrumental and vocal blocks of timbral analogy, built on: trombones and bassoons flutter-tonguing in the lowest register and zarbs tremolo first on the bass, then high; lip tremolo produced with the index finger in the highest vocal range; trumpet multiphonics plus flutter-tonguing in the middle register; lip tremolo achieved by the rapid right-left turning of the head in the highest vocal range, bars 121–123 (Example 21);

ix. That vocal effects replace instrumental effects and instrumental effects replace vocal effects by employing imitative strategies such as the application of tongue clicks instead of the col legno battuto[26] of the strings, and the bowing tremolo on the corpus of the instruments instead of the breath sound (b. 111–113, Example 18);

x. That vocality ensues from the instrumental texture. The acceleration of the rhythmical vocal design in bars 102–106 (Example 13), over crotchets, quavers, triplets, and quintuplets is adopted by the foregoing rhythmisized oscillations of the lower instruments (b. 96–101, Example 17). The instruments embark on polyphonic independent vibrato lines parallel to the rhythmical vocal activity. There exists an immanent expressivity during the passages of hypovibrato and hypervibrato;

xi. Those noise-based sounds, generated by Western classical or unconventional instruments, suggest a textual or a pictorial-to-text-associated reference. Such examples comprise: the percussionist's rubbing of two iron bars (b. 169)[27] and the air noise of the winds, followed by the white noise of the strings[28]. The latter involves the act of exhaling that represents the idea of dying as an acoustical expression of the text's content in an onomatopoetic sense as with Kyprianos's dying breath (b. 178–179);

xii. That as a consequence of musical interpretation, immanently accessible theatrical capacities shift towards the foreground, as shown by the rhythmical hand clapping progression, the powerful flinging of a large glass bottle against an iron plate, the pressing of the bow-hair on the body of the instrument at the very beginning of the work (strings, b. 1–4), and permanently in the course of vocal insertions;

---

[26] Striking the instrument with the wood of the bow from above the string.

[27] Equivalent to the notion of sharpening a knife, which stands for a semantic sound connoting a threatening gesture.

[28] Corresponding to the breathing process.

xiii. That in bars 79–81, in contrast to the hitherto applied tone colour of strings, the sudden and non-recurring electric amplification of the double basses, bowed at the frog, initiates a new timbre effect. The necessity for amplification becomes apparent from the vibrant milieu of fifty whistles, castanets, sonic horn, ratchet, tambourine with jingles, horns, and trombones playing forte to fortississimo.

Such a complex non-hierarchical organization, whose line of development is predictably limited, is neither the result of a pre-arranged formal model or of a ready-made plan. The music accrues on a manifold network of interrelated structures that are, due to their complexity, prima facie opaque. Mobility and openness, rather than stability and closure, are emphasized. Based on an open-ended conception and on the perpetually renewable potential of the structures, the emergent structures are characterized by continuous, incremental, and seamless development: the composed timbre functions representatively for the structural responsibility. The moment is not a victim of structure, but acts with its fleetingness as the motor of the entire process. In doing so, the focus does not contain the definitive structural suction. The ungrounded structures are held in suspension and the moment is prolonged.

The shape's contour is seized before the compositional decision, and subsequently becomes meticulously notated. While the fleeting structured moments are assembled, the loss of structural relevance can be perceived painfully. An interesting phenomenon takes place at this juncture: if the structural tension that links the sound fields is dropped or weakened, the cynosure immediately moves on to another plane. Accordingly, the tension translocates between the planes.

In spite of the meticulous notation of all parameters in the score, the impression of a permanent escape from the definiteness of decision emerges. The inclination of adumbrating and instantly abandoning things occurs throughout, from the first drafts up to the ending of the work. Comparably, the musicalization of the text materializes in close proximity with and concurrently detached from the literary source. This yields provoking contradictions. The sound events, in which the homogeneous gesture dominates, unfold in the interstices. They oscillate, homologously to a virtual loudspeaker, between the worlds of word, image, and sound. In Michaelides's verses 181–190, a poly-pictographic sequence is constructed through the fleeting antithetical images of massacre, blood, small watercourse, billy goats, aging poplar, and 300 new sprouts, ploughing the earth, armed combatants, and peaceful bishops. In short, sound is expressed as an intensification and accumulation of words and images.

Example 18: *Akanthai*, b. 108–113

Mobility within the sound space evolves infrequently through the pitch configuration, due to the material's diversity and inhomogeneous qualities. Therefore, proceeding with absolute pitches imposes a limited or irrelevant methodology vis-à-vis the construction of a mostly homophonic movement. As already observed, the coherence between elements is generated through processual analogy, and not by substance. The production of analogies is a method that triggers non-uniform motion, while the synthesis of such movements propels the development of a spatiotemporal continuum.

A process of multifaceted juxtaposition and superimposition of sounds replaces the traditional notes setting in the score. By dint of implication and parallel existence of pitches with organic, artificial, noise, and electronic sounds, the primacy of pitch is relativized. Hence, the ratio between the priorities of sounding and silence settle the central field of tension.

The expansion in the interior of the structure is essential. The differentiation of the versatile sound plasticity succeeds in the microsphere, whose enlarged reflection is the complex movement of the entire composition. In this regard, by virtue of the soloistic treatment of the parts, the sound apparatus behaves similarly to a centipede: the tension changes permanently between utmost individualization and maximal integration of single elements. Both the high information density and the velocity of succession of the extremely short sound events repeatedly require from the interpreter an expeditious transition from one moment to the next. For example, a shift transpires from the significant foreground to the immense degree of diversity within the fluctuating areas.

To illustrate the facet of mobility involving textual citation, instrumental structures, and vocal topoi in *Akanthai*, I will adduce one explicit place where the orchestra mutates into an absolute chant formation: bar 132 (Example 16). At this juncture, an isolated verse is fragmented, partially alienated, and diversified:

> Spoken with increasing enthusiasm (<u>Three</u> <u>hun</u> - <u>dred</u> <u>new</u> <u>spou</u>-) → imitation of shooting noise ([<u>u</u>]<u>ts</u>) → continuing the beginning's mood (<u>shoo</u>-) → strong accented "<u>t</u>" with pressed air → shout strongly, secco (<u>up</u>).

It is evident that the language elements become materialized into a musicalized purpose like the soundwise expression of shooting that precedes the word "shoot", and placed on the syllable "[u]ts." Further on, the nuances on "t" and "up" pulverize the semantic property of their literary context, and convert it into an instrumental-orientated and explosive auditory expression. The dismantling and explosive gesture is understood as an acoustic transfer or consequence of Michaelides's words "new" and "shoot". A textual-instrumental interface emanates from the vocality that is composed at that point of intersection where the text and instrumental idiom converge.

In bars 102–106, "Three hundred new sprouts shoot up," and "But... when the aging poplar is cut down," and bars 170–177, "The share," the textual fragmentation is prerequisite, and not consequential, though this operation does not remain consistent. During the work's blueprint, the inner gesture of composing was extrovertedly directed, and not conversely. The fragment loses its connection with the source, resulting in the interruption of the text's continuity. The outcome establishes a transfer of creative drive on the peripheral, but absolute corporeality of sound. Ergo, the continuum emerges between the planes of the literary text and organized sound; in one and the same plane manifests discontinuity.

Bar 132 functions as the generative nucleus for the successive two bars. Upon analysis, the aesthetic properties of the vocal sequence together with the preceding and succeeding instrumental constellations display interactive contiguity. The individual tempo indication "as fast as possible" for vocality (b. 132) stands in close correlation with the pizzicato in the strings (b. 139–142) in contrast to the accurately (winds: b. 124–131, winds/percussion/piano: b. 135–138) and spatially/freely notated (vocality: b. 133) polyrhythmic passages. Moreover, the vocal part and strings' episodes consist of homogeneous material with comparable dynamics. With respect to harmonic practice, variegated cluster-like textures occur:

i. In bars 124–131, the winds create a microtonal cluster in vertical and horizontal space;

ii. In bars 132–134, due to the individual pitch levels of the male and female voices of the orchestral musicians, the vocal monophony forms a homophonic timbral cluster;

iii. In bars 135–138, the orchestral passage is initially built horizontally on tone clusters, and thereafter vertically on a chord comprising pitches of a chromatic scale;

iv. In bars 139–142, once the first bar of each string part is repeated, transpositions of horizontally widespread tone clusters are shaped. In performance, however, the dashed barlines are abolished causing intersections.

2.1.6 The Varying Conditions of Integration and Individualization

The strategy of implicating chant segments into instrumental music is situated in the varying condition of individualization and integration. Vocal elements render a collective accent; otherwise the instrumental parts are acutely individualized. Consequently, the vocal application in *Akanthai* is treated:

i. As constant voluminous mass in rhythmical unison (b. 88–92, 102–106, 122–123, 134);

ii. In rhythmical unison (b. 102–106) and in synchronous secco moments (b. 90–92) with the instruments;

iii. With gradually increasing mass (b. 170–177);

iv. As organized mass in chaotic motion (b. 132–133);

v. In high-density disparity (b. 88–92) as well as concurrently antithetical tempo and rhythmic figuration (accelerando / ritardando, b. 118) with the instruments;

vi. Surrounded by polyphonic instrumental textures (b. 88–92, 102–106, 170–177);

vii. Infiltrated into a linear instrumental sequence (b. 111–113);

viii. In timbral dialogue with the instruments (b. 122–123);

ix. In kinetic friction with the orchestral sound (b. 170–176).

The characteristic vocality is always implemented homophonically or monophonically with multiple voices and indefinite pitch. This tactic reverts back to the plausible conundrum that the instrumentalists might hesitate to perform any extra-instrumental components, or without the expected vocal-expressive qualities. For these reasons it is legitimate to appoint a separate, professional speaking choir. The work's initial intention, however, will be contrastingly exposed, acoustically and theatrically, inciting a falsification. An extra speaking choir next to the orchestra gains a different interpretational form and perceptual appearance for the piece.

Bernd Alois Zimmermann anticipated, prior to the premiere of *Antiphonen*, that the integrated speaking passages would instigate protests. He still considered it as appropriate material, because the use of language arose out of the climax of the antiphonal principle: at that place where the apogee of the viola soloist is achieved, the action of the orchestral musicians is juxtaposed by that of language.

As for the propriety of the collective spoken passages in *Akanthai*, with reference to the courageous attitude of Archbishop Kyprianos in Michaelides's verses, and reminiscent of the major chorus temperament in the ancient plays of Aeschylus, it is possible to interpret it as assuming the role of a decisive and resistive demonstrating crowd. This propounds a testimonial in a momentary flashback, whereby humanistic engagement has an effect on the work's emotional disposition. Although the verbal insertions set semantically accentuated points in the music, the hidden motive does not emerge directly. Their context becomes allegorical; the quotation remains arcane. Since music expresses autonomously a rich contrasted network of gestures, the actual motive of the poem naturally adopts a more general perspective.

The concluding sequence of "The share" begins immediately after the percussion solo of two iron bars rubbed together (b. 169). By use of artistic license, this action serves as an acoustic metaphor for the execution of Kyprianos.[29] In the following bars, the polyrhythmic structure in staccato articulation of the instrumental tableau, with the vocal ostinati woven in between, causes an interfacial tension (b. 170–177, Example 15). The resultant vocal-instrumental interaction, with the contributing groups gradually growing in size and the voices emotionally electrifying the episode, is an evocative rendition of the reaction pertaining to the sentence of Kyprianos. The energy charge of the execution scene is reflected by the instrumental sound, while the continuous repetition of "The share" of the chorus emphasizes the momentousness of the event.

2.1.7 The Polydimensional Articulation of Homogeneity

The articulation of homogeneity in *Akanthai* is polydimensional. This is to differentiate between parallel and horizontally progressed homogeneity. The parallel plane suggests a sequence of consecutive and single sound objects (e.g. b. 68 and b. 110–111, Example 18). The horizontal plane is then developed within a successively synthesized polyphonic context, as at the very beginning of the composition, where the bow-hair of the strings is pressed on the instruments' backs, and rubbed with velocity-varied rotations of the wrist (b. 1–4, Example 19).

A stretched form of simultaneous parallel and horizontal homogeneity exists in bars 164–168 (Example 20). In this case, the flutes' triad constellation depends on a subtraction and abstraction of its consisting notes (F♯ / E → D♯ ↔ D♮ /

---

[29] Such artistically created sonic icons are subjective, and function only within the dream world that memory produces; compare the memory concept in the literature of Marcel Proust.

A → B ↔ C). While the pitch is kept at a steady note value, the enharmonic variations, E 1–2–3, deviate from equal tempered tuning. Likewise, though with a different set of harmonically related notes, fixed quarter-tone chords with individual enharmonic changes, the trombones' progression unfolds. Moreover, the timbre of the amplified cimbalom in percussion 2 stands in an imitative relationship with the pizzicati sul ponticello (violoncello 4–6, contrabass) and the pizzicati that are either performed ordinary or behind the bridge (violin I–II, viola, violoncello 1–3), so demonstrating a homogeneous mixture.

Two types of imitation form the homogeneous structure:

> The introductory passage of the strings depends on timbral mimesis, in the sense of exact replication, and on an imitative pattern: violas' dux.[30] The latter is the generating sound cell.
>
> And
>
> The generating sound cell is onwards represented. Simulations take on modes of representation that are not so literal. To put it another way, simulations are dynamic constructs of representation. I call this procedural representation. The term "procedural" is shorthand for the process-based ways that sounds can signify. The sonic character of the strings is depicted on percussion with the friction drum and big paper cement bag, on piano with the rubbing of the lowest string, on trumpets with multifrequence or distorted tone, and on bass clarinet with the spread or broken note, a form of distortion produced by simultaneous non-harmonic pitches. Subsequently, the inflowing block-like structure of the winds, a micropolyphonic surface shaded with air noise, blown with flutter-tonguing and tremolo though instruments in bars 5 and 6, attempts to imitate the effect of the strings.

The opening of *Akanthai* is subject to an additional type of imitation: a rhythmical canon (strings, percussion 2; comes 1–6).

An examination of the percussion solo of rubbing two iron bars together in bar 169, and the score's adjoining sound constituents at the beginning of section E (b. 154 et seq.), reveals a variety of analogous relationships: the violins and violas alternate in rapid glissando shiftings dovetailing with the tremoli (b. 154–156^1, though preceded at the end of section D in b. 150 and 152), the gradually multiplied lines of violins I (1 → 1–3 → 1–6 → 1–9 → tutti), violins II (1 → 1–2 → 1–3 → 1–7 → tutti), violas (1 → 1–2 → tutti), and violoncellos

---

[30] In the contrapunctal technique of canon the initial melody is called dux (the leader) and the imitative melody, which is played in a different voice, comes (the follower).

(1 → 1–2 → 1–3), the tremoli of piccolo wood-blocks and amplified cimbalom, the trilled sound of flexaton, and part of the wind section that changes enharmonically (b. 156^2–161). Even though these elements are not aligned successively in the score in terms of a timbral sequence, they have been either vertically interleaved or positioned horizontally apart.

Example 19: *Akanthai*, b. 1–6

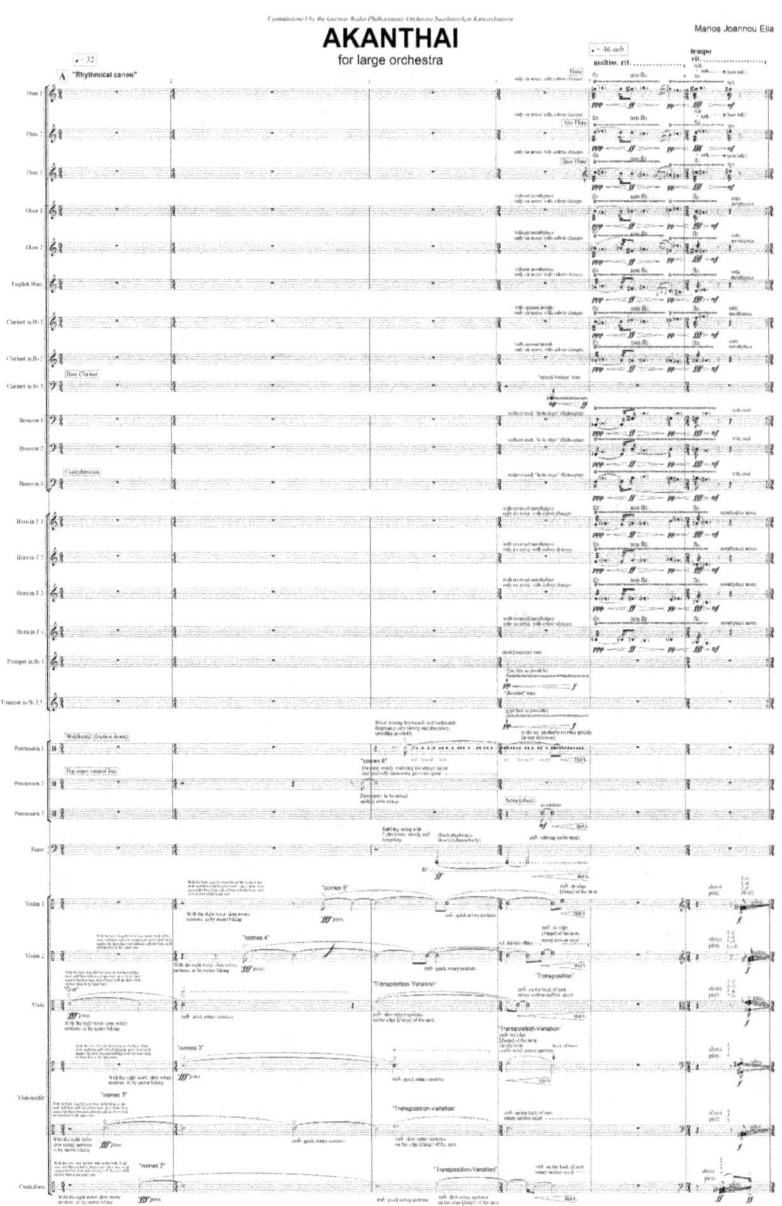

Example 20: *Akanthai*, b. 162–169

The customized formation as well as the integration of vocality into the orchestral structures evolves in the light of mimesis. By way of example, the individual tempo marking "as fast as possible" is an indication of the vocal passage in bars 132–133 (Example 16), which is later applied to the strings (b. 139–142). Comparing the structure of these extracts, a form of musematic repetition is common for both sections.[31] In *Akanthai*'s case, the minimal unit consists of a bar's material as a module, used to generate a structural framework. Notwithstanding that the same material is iterated, each repetition is slightly differentiated: the content-related parameters are manipulated. The duplicated bars are not identical, but similar, and therefore they do not remain precisely the same; reshaping *Akanthai* from chamber to large orchestra conformed to this principle. Imitation takes place within the context of the reproductive process. Thus, repetition is reflected with the intention of imitation.

Referring to the second mimetic type, procedural representation, another section that contains an imitative interaction between instrumental and vocal sounds occurs in bars 121^2–123, at which point a spatiotemporal crossover between the two emerges (Example 21). The horn multiphonics with the instrument's bell on snare drum's surface subsists in relation to the performance of the trumpets on water's surface. Equivalent to horns and trumpets, the lip tremolo using the index finger and the lip tremolo supported by rapid turnings of the head to either side achieve an associated effect. The vocal-instrumental progression is initiated by the hybridization of flutter-tonguing on bassoons and trombones, together with the tremoli on zarbs. The intention is to create a uniform amalgam between both sections, and to achieve a variation of the character of horns. The transitions at this juxtaposition pass through the entire ambitus like a flash from extremely low in the bassoons and trombones to the horns and trumpets in the middle and on to the voice in the highest position.

For producing a catalyst between heterogeneous materials, the same procedure links the score's previous succession (b. 119–120, Example 21): the vocal effect of tongue clicks signifies a relationship between the col legno battuto of the strings and the high-pitched sound of the zarb. Hence, it follows that vocality functions as the pivotal point of transition between two discrete instrumental timbres at the end of the decrescendo in the strings and the beginning of the crescendo in the zarbs. Similarly, the timbre associated with tongue clicks is the balloons bursting to mark the turn to a contradistinctive section (b. 123).

---

[31] A museme is the smallest unit embodying meaning in music, analogous to a morpheme, which is "the smallest semantically meaningful unit in a language," (Sternberg, *Cognitive Psychology*, p. 363).

Akanthai ends with a three-voice progression of blowing air without pitch through the wind instruments, violins and violas bowing on bridge to create white noise, and violoncellos and double basses bowing on the instrument's corpus (b. 178–179). These sounds stand together in a direct mimesis, in a sound colour liaison, but also in timbral connection with the whispering nuance of the voices at the entry of "The Share."

Regarding the content of the last three passages (b. 119–120, 121^2–123, 178–179), all sounds are developed entirely by extended techniques. Unconventional, unorthodox, or non-traditional skills of voice and instrument playing produce sonorous-expressive unities. The compositional process with tones was replaced by a synthetic course of action consisting of an expanded repertoire. It is not the pitches or ratios of the chords, but the ratio between the manifold sonic events, their linked interaction, and contrast degree, which settle the poles of composition. The work's focus is determined not only by the sonic result, but to a greater degree by the concrete situation of the substantive and energetic conditions of the work's repertoire. In this particular context, as a result of exploiting versatile imitation-based practices and manifestations of imitation in individual behaviours, the model of homogeneous gesture dominates, interlocking a series of heterogeneous microsounds, and developing polyphonic formations as well as a linear continuum. Singular components merge into one another. At the same time, a beatless, flowing feeling ensues, acting as a link between sequential sound spheres.

Even if this commentary mostly concentrates on musical materials that represent a deviation from traditional practice, it must be underlined that harmonic concepts are concomitantly present. To deviate from deviation itself, a purely harmonic structural field follows a purely unconventional topos of timbral organization in which they coexist (e.g. Example 14 and 16; Example 11 and 20).

Example 21: *Akanthai*, b. 119–123

The vocal insertions are predominantly monophonic. The same motif is duplicated, effecting a collective synchronized action. Synchronization, which implies homorhythm, renders an optimized homogeneous topology in the music. In the following, a close analysis of two score excerpts explicates certain aspects of monophony; concurrently, the study comments on a series of issues concerning the employment of vocal interjections and their impact within the instrumental setting.

The first extensive vocal sequence is in section C (bars 88–92; Example 17). The concerted structure consists of four layers: horns, trumpets, trombones, and chant. All instrumental groups are linearly evolved on a duplication mode, either in a homophonic, or in an enharmonically varied relationship. Each instrumental line, nevertheless, possesses a soloistic design, since the muted and unmuted indications as well as the enharmonic changes are individually composed. The polyrhythmic phrasings of horns and trumpets require personal interpretation.

Monophonic notation transubstantiates, through the process of interpretation, into a homophonic mass of sound: all monophonic vocal passages are notated with an indefinite pitch, connoting that their performance depends on everyone's speaking pitch level, male and female. That is why the speaking choir does not become manifested in unison, but emerges on the basis of a timbral chant cluster. A similar phenomenon arises when several wind instruments execute simultaneously individual air sounds on indefinite pitches (b. 108–110; Example 18). Consequently, a kind of composed improvisation becomes an inherent feature of interpretation.

In the above-mentioned excerpt, Kyprianos offers the rudiments for the incurrence of percussive-like vocality. The sounds and syllables "[k]y – prrri, a – a – a – a – a, nos! nos! nos!" are split apart within the space of five bars. The graphemes of the word are fragmented and separately musicalized. Despite their fragmentation and partly repetitive components, the semantic continuation is not dropped because the graphemes' order is retained. It is more likely that the phonemes are remodelled, that is, the word's segmental units of sound are employed in order to form, de novo, a musico-dramatic expression.

The process of reciprocal action between the vocal and instrumental groups involves the method of procedural representation. The rolled "r" stands as an analogue to the flutter-tonguing and tremolo in the winds. Syllables and single vowels are mainly appointed as short, dry moments, always in a vertical synchronization with instruments, which brings to mind secco recitative. The sequence's climax ends with a tutti dynamic accent of the vocal and instrumental forces. Only then, a double wah-wah tube vibrato in percussion 1 and

3 elicits a contrasting component; this is the liaison module between Kyprianos and the following echo progression that retains the secco character (b. 93–96).

Throughout the Kyprianos passage, the formation of the vocal part is comprised of two regularly repetitive sound cells: "a" and "nos!" Repetition can be understood as a duplication of the material in the horizontal axe, as a horizontally shifted monophony. It is graphically visible by adjusting the score's orientation from to landscape.

Temporal regularity is suspended however, due to the sequential indications of sempre molto accelerando → tempo → accelerando sempre. A similar spatio-temporal shift unfolds in the duplicated major second interval of horns in bars 89^2–89^6. During the repetitions of the triplet figure, the duration of every flutter-tongued note lasts a semiquaver longer than its precedecessor. Analysis of the harmonic superstructure above the duplicated linear line discloses a homophonic texture, consisting of a coexisting minor and major second, as well as minor and major third. The major second interval is designed with alternating stopped and open notes (+/o). Additionally, the linear plane is ornamented with trills that consist of a pulsating oscillation between minor and major thirds apart (C♯$_5$ / E$_5$, B$_4$ / G♯$_4$, C$_5$ / G♯$_4$ [A♯$_4$]).

Employing the technique of hand-stopping for the French horns, and mutes for the other brass instruments, effects the modification of timbre and pitch: the sound is not projected through the bell but through the vibrating tube, which darkens the timbre and raises the pitch by a minor second. The closing of bell or mute associates phonetically with the stop or plosive consonants, such as "B(ut)" or "p(o)p(lar)." The opening correlates with the vowels that are pronounced with an agape vocal tract.

The second score excerpt is made up of a stylized recitative succession based on the verse "But (…) when the aging poplar is cut down" (b. 102–106, Example 13). In terms of the clerical derivation of Archbishop Kyprianos, the core principle of repetition is mirrored in a form of mystical prayer called Hesychasm. In the Orthodox Church, Hesychasm includes a continual repetition of the Jesus Prayer. Via repetition, the Michaelides's verse in *Akanthai* obtains a certain stillness and emptiness. By modifying the sound parameters of the recurring textual elements, equilibrium is achieved.

In musicalizing the verse's syllables, an artificially vocalized form of verbal expression is evoked. In the course of recirculation, units of the verse are gradually omitted. In that way, the focus is shifted towards the inside by saying "[But]…when the a-ging pop-lar is cut do-wn/ when the a-ging pop-lar is cut do-wn/ a-ging pop-lar is cut do-wn/ –lar is cut do-wn."

Dismembering the building blocks of language, the words, in addition to the irregular rhythmical patterns, result in the suspension of the stress of the syllables. Hence, the speaking choir stresses atonal syllables or rhythms of unequal metre, a facet that also transpires in some Cypriot demotic songs. The whole issue is further exaggerated by the accentuated mark on every syllable and beat respectively, together with the superimposed dynamics. Syllables are treated as distinct sound units analogous to instrumental tones. In this case, the idiosyncratic sound, rather than the concrete pitch, is quintessential.

In *Akanthai*, as well as in other compositions like *Die Jagd*, the affinity of repeating single phonemes, vowels or consonants, syllables, words or verses, corresponds to the rhyme notion derived from homeoteleuton. Homeoteleuton, first identified by Aristotle in his *Rhetoric*, is a rhyme technique that denotes repetition of endings in words.

Likewise in the poem of Michaelides, the third and fourth verses end with a perfect rhyme with the stress on the penultimate syllable of the words, where the latter phonetic is identical.[32] Since the rhymes sound the same, they are homogeneous. In respect to the musical nature of rhyme, attention is transferred from the semantic content of the words to a criterion of purely acoustic linkage. As a consequence, the rhyme has a sense of abstraction, which can be musically taken advantage of. This characteristic is extensively exploited by Cypriot folk music. For instance, the song *Three Olives and One Tomato* uses the first verse only as an auditory rhyme with the second or third. A linguistically meaningful connection simply does not exist: "Three olives and one tomato, I love a woman with black eyes."[33] Interestingly, the flow of the lyric is kept consistent throughout the entire song, so that the first verse always rhymes with the second or third, and all of the first lines of the rhyming couplets are interlinked with one another: "Three olives and one pepper, I love her but she doesn't know it, that we will become a pair."[34] The rhyming material that usually consists of one to three syllables is comparable to the concept of sound object. To this extent, within a polyphonic instrumental diversity, the monophonic repetition of the phonemes in *Akanthai*, as in the (Kypri)-a-nos's passage, materializes in the sense of acoustic correspondence.

---

[32] Θαρκέται and καταλυέται.

[33] Τρεις ελιές τζιαι μιαν τομάταν, αγαπώ μιαν μαυρομμάταν.

[34] Τρεις ελιές τζ' έναν πιπέριν, αγαπώ την τζ' εν το ξέρει, πως εννά γινούμεν ταίριν.

2.1.8 Conclusion

Once a musical composition makes use of a literary source, the general discussion of musico-literary intermediality is raised. However, there is no intermedial relationship between the initial text and the one used in the musical piece. The specific standpoint signifies that the medium of text is represented by the medium of music, since, in the progress of transformational intermediality, the medium of text appears at first throughout the composition's score and subsequently the composition's performance in order to manifest. In other words, the text is an integral component of the music by which it is represented. Insofar as the music is not a bearer of an intermedial relationship, it referentially points to the literary text. Essential differences make it possible to define the dissimilarities between the representing and the represented medium. These differences epitomize a transformation that can be ontologically determined by the composition's morphological consistency.

According to the remarks in the score, all transitions should be very discreet, with rapid changes from one sound event to the next. Special attention is to be given to the coordination of sound and silence within a sense of unfading hovering. Seeing that the instrumental and vocal microstructures continuously and subtly change their timbre, they are elaborately notated and designated with detailed explanations, densely differentiated, nuanced and entangled; the distinguishing clarity could be thwarted in several places. In addition, *Akanthai* achieves the impression of fragility, thereby obtaining a reinforced pronunciation. This is accomplished via the application of both traditional and extended instrumental techniques, extra-instrumental apparatuses such as sonic horn, mouth organs, whistles, and horns playing with the bell above the surface of a snare drum, unconventional percussion materials such as friction drum, waterphone, bullroarer, bottle smash, wooden and aluminium wardrobe doors slamming, the auxiliary acoustical actions such as hand clapping, electric amplification, as well as the vocality components of chant in disparate formations and vocal extended techniques.

Due to its heterogeneity, *Akanthai*'s repertoire implies a deviation from conventional orchestral instrumentation. The encompassing elements converge via intercommunication and mutual influence into a unified whole. This unifying total consciousness is linked to the concept of polyaesthetics. Derived from the Aristotelian notion of sensorium commune,[35] polyaesthetics is understood here

---

[35] Aristotle distinguishes between objects that are directly perceptible by a single and by any and all of the senses. Colour for sight and sounds for hearing are examples of the former; there is, however, no sense to perceive movement or rest, but the movement of an object can be perceived either by sight or hearing. These properties are common to all the senses.

only within the compositional context, in terms of the work's polymedial content; the sensory perception and cognitive reception of music are completely excluded. Concerning the prefix poly, this does not denote a quantitative, but a qualitative paradigm shift: not a quantitative much, but a qualitative more. In the broadest sense, regardless of the media quantity and the amount of extraneous materials, the meaningful ratio between the conventional orchestral and unconventional, non-orchestral elements plays the central role.

Akanthai partially retains the presence of the four verses of *The 9th of July 1821*. The unexpected flickering and quick disappearance of verbal insertions concern the technique applied to heighten dramatic tension, as well as to convey the concealed text and subtext. Yet, in the majority of cases, the music advances as a carrier of an autonomous dramaturgical expressiveness: the longer the words remain absent, the more the tension escalates. The apparent loss of certainties, such as the semantics of the text, is compensated by an increase in aesthetic complexity in terms of musical production. Within an invisible and multidimensional acoustic space emerges the enactment of drama. Hence, the bottom line is that the envelopment of the text serves the revelation of the music.

Music gains in directness because of the lack of confidence in the self-control of time while my own time is carried as if guided by a sense of fatalism. This is why there is no formal plan before the compositional practice. The fleetingness and volatility of the moment is the driving force of the entire compositional process while the focalizing perspective permanently fluctuates between the structural layers and the textual reference. Being perpetually in motion involves staying and resting in tandem, so that in spite of the high rate density and the renewal potential of the sound events, the result – reminiscent of the static solemnity of Byzantine icons – is located on the meta-level of the sense of time.

2.2 The Situative Conditions Resulting from the Abrupt Omission of the Relationship to the Literary Source on the Basis of Exemplary Excerpts from the Opera *Die Jagd*

There are several places in the music where the relationship to the literary source is entirely omitted, where an associated musico-literary idea is completed purely for the benefit of musical creation.

A concrete literary character trait or component unit evokes either the first musical motif or acoustical idea of a texture, or a new extra-musical or programmatic impulse, from where the core motif or fundamental sound module is introduced. In the first case, music and text are placed on the opposite ends of a scale; the compositional process devises various ways to traverse that scale. In the second case, the particular motif or sound module functions as a window that displaces the focus from outside the literary frame of reference. The momentary abandonment of the text is completed by the inserted musical opening, and is then followed by the return to the text, at which juncture the order of events narrated in the literary source continues.

In a similar approach to the second case, the plot of Wolfgang Amadeus Mozart's opera buffa *Le nozze di Figaro* is diverted by an aria. At supposedly insignificant occasions in the opera, like the Susanna's aria "Venite, inginocchiatevi," Mozart has created a space for the objective of a solo part while Susanna combs the hair of Cherubino. Susanna's aria not only describes single affects or emotions, but also articulates physical acting and interacting. Mozart repeatedly sets prosaic processes to music, like the measuring of a room, the disguising of the page, the writing of a letter, and the seeking of a needle.

In Baroque opera, the aria is a self-contained musical unit: the composer's response to both the dramatic situation and the librettist's formal choices with the text. In addition to recitative, Claudio Monteverdi introduced the aria as a more lyrical type of monody, a medium thought to approximate the singing of the ancient Greek theatre. Whereas a recitative advances the plot, an aria usually brings the action to a halt. And while a recitative often involves a rapid delivery of the text, an aria works through the text at a more leisurely pace.[36]

The opera *Die Jagd* (2008),[37] written for coloratura soprano, boy soprano, countertenor and bass, three actors, juvenile vocal ensemble, two speaking choirs, twenty recorded voices, instrumental ensemble in two groups, car sextet and electronics, is based on an original libretto in German by Marianne Frei-

---

[36] Words are repeated and vowels are extended by means of vocal melismas.
[37] The Hunt.

dig and Andreas Liebmann; however, numerous musical structures were composed prior to the existence of any textual references. Furthermore, the operatic work possesses a broad spectrum of original ideas beyond the libretto. In this regard, the present section concentrates on the analysis of some paradigmatic features and fundamental production mechanisms of the music generated out of the libretto. At the same time, the analysis elucidates certain processes of transition from one medium to the other, and delineates the methodological course of action concerning the musical openings.

Die Jagd's script galvanized the invention of multifarious extra-textual elements. Commencing with the libretto's description of the woodland in Scene IV, "Geräusche," it proceeds in the manner of an inverted depiction of "how the *birds* creek, and the *trees* sing."[38] This bizarre description instigated the formation of the juvenile vocal ensemble of female vocal quartet plus two male speaking voices, thereby embodying the hunting choir (Jagdchor).

In the same scene, an auxiliary chant ensemble is notated in the score as the woodland tribe (Waldvolk). Because the woodland tribe was not part of the libretto's conception, its actual presence is reserved and imaginatively articulated through the music. Due to the unfeasible inclusion of a separate large speaking choir at the work's premiere, a group of instrumentalists functioned as the chant ensemble. Its appearance is situated in the middle of the scene (b. 67–72, Example 22), equivalent to the encounter of the tribe in the middle of the forest. At this point, the chant ensemble is blended with the juvenile vocal ensemble. Their vocal behaviour is instrumentally treated, although they proceed differently. Each one has a strict homophonous architecture that interweaves with the percussion and brass. Analysis of the involved groups shows that they are mutually composed in a percussive way: the strong inhalations and exhalations of the chant ensemble stand in rhythmic and timbral relationship with the air blown through the brass instruments resembling a damp machine (b. 67–68^1). Concurrently, the juvenile vocal ensemble (indicated in the score as Vok 1–2–3–4) implements a downwards and upwards figure in alternation (ta≡ka / to≡ko, te≡ke / ti≡ki), while the percussionists execute either scraping-tremoli on small and Turkish cymbal, Chinese and Wuhan tam-tam, or rub together two sandpaper blocks with resonant boxes.

In bars 68^2–71 there is a polyrhythmic progression, which consists of the aforementioned four layers: chant ensemble, juvenile vocal ensemble, percussion, and brass. Atypically, the chant ensemble, this time a woodland tribe, is transformed into a corporal percussive group, carrying out hand clapping and foot stomping with the heels clumping on resonating wood boards. This corre-

---

[38] Wie die Vögel knirschen, und die Bäume singen.

sponds to the Maori haka, a form of communication, which maximizes the corporeality of language. Haka is a genre of vociferated text accompanied by vigorous body movements in which the differing parts of the body represent the diverse instruments. A timbral cocktail of the corporal sounds materializes when the first percussionist does a marching men effect with a wooden marching machine, while the second strikes membranophones or hits two drumsticks together.

Even though two superimposed sequences of elements share a common set of parameters, they occur independently.[39] Without letting the individual sound object identities dissolve, a hybridized acoustical outcome is produced. Moreover, the coexisting juvenile vocal ensemble is intertwined with the overall concoction of sounds, primarily because they occupy the same locality in the score. The juvenile vocal ensemble with capricious microstructural elements possesses an individual material and configuration in comparison to the others, so that, via differentiation and collocation of heterogeneous planes, a separate form of connectivity is attained.

Looking more closely at the structure, however, it becomes apparent that a series of communicative procedures link the juvenile vocal ensemble to the rest planes. The "Ha" of the juvenile vocal ensemble interacts with the chant ensemble's line of inhaling and exhaling, as well as with the brass's sequence of air sounds. Some lips tremoli appear synchronous with the snare drum tremoli. The juvenile vocal ensemble's rhythmic profile is built on semiquaver units, and so are the structures of chant ensemble, brass, and percussion.

In view of the chant ensemble's sequence, a horizontal and a vertical aspect determine its configuration. The brass group performs with air sounds a kind of free ostinato throughout the entire passage. This is the horizontal connecting component between the section's first (b. 67–68^1) and second part (b. 68^2–71). The section ends with the question "Wie?"[40] realized on a forceful chant tutti corresponding to the vertical aspect by all instrumentalists and the chant ensemble, except for the juvenile vocal ensemble. At this moment, "Wie?" signifies the completion of the temporarily embedded musical opening. The relation to the libretto is therewith reconstructed. "Wie," without the question mark, is the initiation word of the ensuing verse "Wie die Dachse plätschern,"[41] enunciated by the singing of the characters Andy and Maria.

---

[39] For example, the first sequence consists of hand clapping, snare drum and hitting drumsticks together; the second of foot stomping and tom-tom.

[40] How?

[41] How the badgers gurgle.

Example 22: *Die Jagd*, Scene IV, "Geräusche," b. 67–72

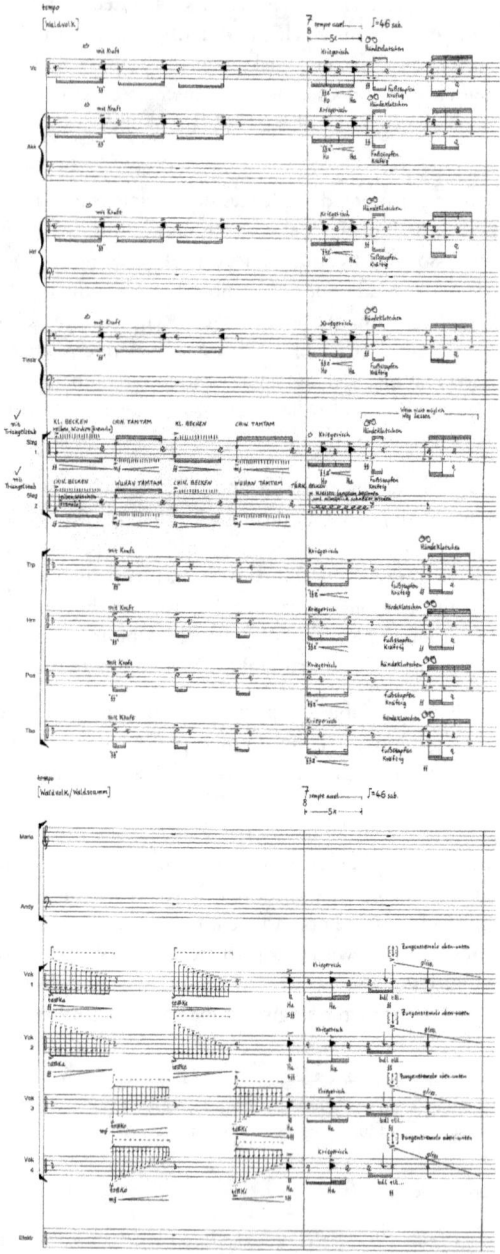

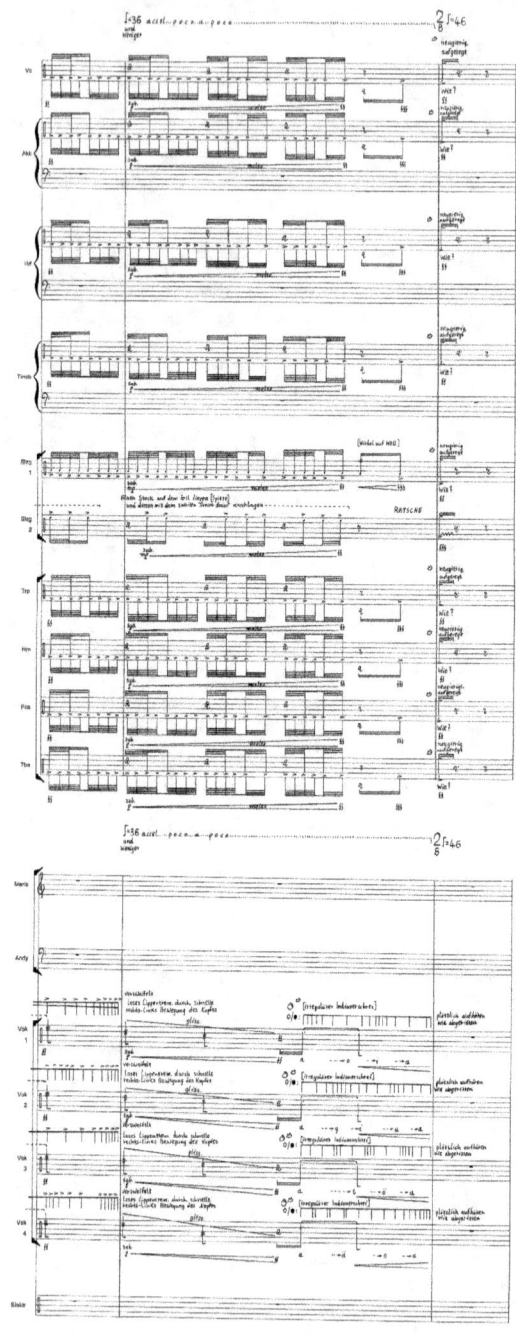

An ensemble of six cars – Aston Martin DB9 Volante, Jaguar XKR, Ford Shelby Mustang, Ford Focus ST, Volvo S80, and Land Rover Defender – establishes an extraordinary apparatus in the conception of *Die Jagd*. This peculiar formation is exploited both instrumentally and visually. Sounds, such as the running motor engine with varied pressure on the accelerator,[42] the car horn, and the opening and closing of car doors, in addition to automotive lighting, like the night and stop light, the headlamp, or the directional indicators (Scene II, "Nacht, Damals (A)," "LICHTMUSIK"), count among the material components employed in the opera. The implication of cars has a contextual and conceptual status in the plot. Based on the technologized description of the forest, its artificial nature, and its transformational changes depicted in the libretto (Scene IV, "Geräusche," Example 23), the car ensemble represents forest creatures (Waldwesen).

Example 23: *Die Jagd*, Scene IV, "Geräusche," libretto

> Andy: Komm, wir machen einen Waldspaziergang.
>
> Maria: Unglaublich, wie die Vögel knirschen.
>
> Andy & Maria: Wie die Gräser heulen.
> Wie die Dachse plätschern. Wie
> die Bächlein quieken.
>
> Maria: Wie die Füchse knacken.
> Wie Äste knurren.
>
> Andy: Wie die Dachse plätschern.
> Wie die Bächlein quieken.
> Woher hast du eigentlich deine Phantasie so plötzlich?
>
> Maria: Schon immer.
>
> Andy: Da ist irgendwas neu –
> Wer setzt dir diese Flausen in den Kopf?
> Hast du einen anderen?[43]

---

[42] Tone frequencies commensurate to revolutions per minute.
[43] Andy: Come, let's take a forest walk. – Maria: Unbelievable, how the birds creek. – Andy & Maria: How the grasses howl. How the badgers gurgle. How the streams squeal. – Maria: How the foxes creak. How the branches growl. – Andy: How the badgers gurgle. How the streams squeal. From where do you actually stimulate your fantasy? – Maria: As always. – Andy: There is something new – Who puts a bee in your bonnet? Do you have a lover?

Apart from the hunting choir, the woodland tribe, and the forest creatures, a secondary group, a mixed speaking choir called "Stadtstimmen," appears. Stadtstimmen, the voices of the city, emerge instantly and signify the internal space and the toughts of the central figures, not unlike the ancient Greek chorus. They represent the metaphor of the city, from which the protagonists cannot escape. As the city expands, and the number as well as the intensity of the interpolated voices gradually increases, the more the family inclines towards the attraction of the illusion of nature.

Although the libretto presupposes a singing choir for the twenty city voices, the composition conceives two dissimilar approaches that are optionally combinable: a pre-recorded version of every voice projected via the car speakers and supported acoustically by the spatial loudspeaker system, and/or a legion of spear carriers that emerge in the background.

The dramatis personæ Andy and Maria, and their daughter Isabell are listed and handled as single protagonists in the libretto. At the same time, the plot concerns the antithetical poles of nature and technology, past and present, reality and imagination. To the credit of additive melodramatic complexity, the compositional procedure reflects this bipolarity by doubling the leading roles as a dramaturgical technique: Andy and Maria are simultaneously personified by a singer and an actor. Isabell, however, is portrayed by an actress with no doubling figure. Benni, a boy soprano, is Isabell's brother, with whom he always appears hand in hand. All vocal acting parts, whether singers or actors, are explicitly notated in the score.

The forest's delineation in the libretto lines, as in the "Geräusche" scene, influenced the selection of the instrumentarium. This is coupled with the types of the instruments, their playing methods, and techniques:

i. The peculiar sound scenery of the forest involves instruments like the musical saw, the theremin, the friction drum (Waldteufel), the lion's roar, the outsized cowbell, the flexaton, the bass monochord, assorted types of hand-operated bird calls, the birds' ratchet, the bubbling water effect produced by blowing through a tube immersed in water, or emulated instrumentally by the lowest brass, a superball mallet that is dragged across the head of the bass drum, an upside-down cymbal that is placed upon the drumhead of a pedal timpano and rolled while executing a glissando;

ii. Alternatively, violoncello, accordion, harp, and celesta reproduce birdlike whistling trills (b. 42–43, 44–46) and the trumpet player performs with the bell partially touching the water surface (b. 26);

iii. As previously noted, certain ways of proceeding with the musical material enlighten the high degree of systematic exploration of instruments and objects, regarding their sound possibilities and qualities. Correspondingly, vocally generated actions in the brass section obtain unconventional sounds. In a distinctive manner, for the lowest brass, such examples include the creaking of indefinite pitch over the gradual transition of the phonetic sequence y [according to the tongue position: close front] → ɔ [open-mid back] → u [close back], b. 23, the head voice with rolled "r" (pr, wr, br; b. 28), the whispering tremolo ts≡k (b. 23–24), and the breathed, voiceless impulses tʃi-ki, tʃœ-kœ, tʃo-ko, tʃe-ke, tsa, tso, and tsa (b. 30–33);

iv. Supplemental to the instruments, the atypical sonic palette of the forest encompasses the vocal elements of creaking voices, bird-like lips tremoli, simultaneous breathing and whistling, whistle-trilled glissandi, bilabial and tongue clicks, Amerindian screams, and wah-wah effects;

v. Maria's introduction resembles birdsong (Example 24). The literary substance of the verse "Unglau<u>bl</u>ich, <u>wie</u> <u>die</u> Vögel <u>kni</u>rschen,"[44] is pulverized. This is context-bound: for example, the sounds "l" and "r", surrounded by other words and syllables, sound like the letters "l" and "r"; however, when sung tremolando, surrounded by the polyphonic tremoli of harp, accordion, cimbalom, cembalo, and cello in the high register, they sound like an instrumental element unrelated to language. There are further steps in this scale: the rapid circulation of the syllables "kni-wie-die-bli" is not semantically connected to language. It suggests the twittering of birds while also being linked to the staccatissimo repetitions of the brass whose sound is twisted by the mutes' tremoli. The musical saw or the theremin tends to resemble the human singing voice.

---

[44] How the birds creek! Unbelievable!

Example 24: *Die Jagd*, Scene IV, "Geräusche," Maria's part resembling birdsong, b. 1–14

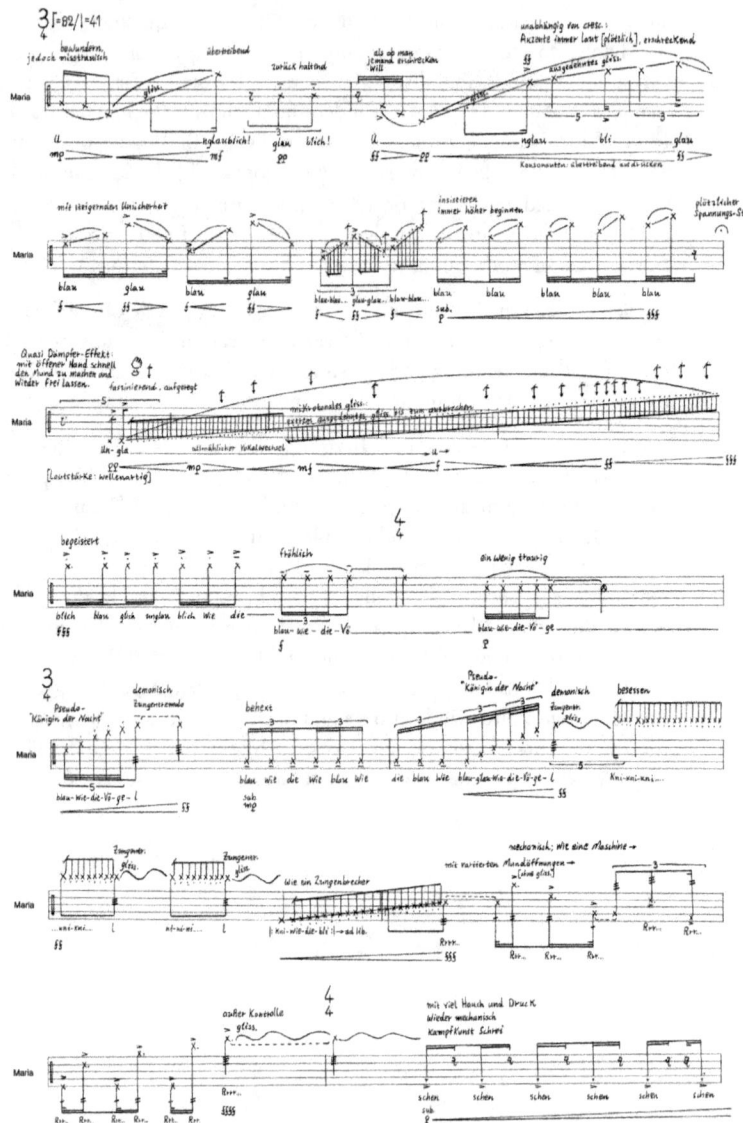

The importance of the associations established between the libretto and the music becomes clear in Scene V, "Nacht, Damals (B)," albeit the compositional development advances self-directed. For the first time, Cem enters the stage but remains voiceless throughout the scene. Cem's silence is denoted in the libretto with a descriptive account of his actions:

> <u>Cem</u> taucht auf. <u>Er läuft</u> in der Garage herum, und prüft auch mal ein Auto, indem er sich reinsetzt, <u>und</u> aufs Gas <u>drückt</u>.[45]

Cem is the character who simultaneously impersonates the role of the car dealer on the plane of reality and the devil/seducer within the imaginative world. His name, comparable to the names of Kyprianos in *Akanthai* (b. 88–92) and Zhedros, Zakos, Drakos, Lenas in *Thalatta, Thalatta!* (b. 63), provides the textual material for a quasi-onomatopoetic progression. Because Cem has a direct relationship to the automobiles, the onomatopoetic reference suggests the acoustic impression of a motor engine, produced by the choral chanting of sounds such as the percussive attacks over "CEM – m-m-m m – CEM – m – CEM" (Example 25).

The figure of Cem is additionally depicted by the brass quartet and the metal percussion instruments, metal serving as a representation of the automobiles.[46] The brass quartet opens Scene V, prior to the Cem-Chant sequence and incessantly accompanies Cem over the entire work, as in Scene XIV, "Isas Jagd" (b. 153/154).[47] Subsequent to the Cem-Chant the brass quartet has a short interlude, and the scene continues to a new chanting consecution of equal length: "Er läuft … und drückt […]" (b. 38–51, Example 26). At this point, the above-mentioned scenic commentary of the libretto, the stage directions, become compositionally essential. Inspired by machinery and mechanical processes, the text is thereby newly moulded as in bars 38–54 when "[e]r läuft – und – drückt […] drü-drück – drü_ck – tü-drü-tü – drückütück" along with its phonemic variation "ru-ru-ru – dru-cku-tuck" occurs.

By signifying Cem's identity, the functional perspective of the choral chant is to provide information relevant to the plot. This is reminiscent of the ancient Greek chorus, which expresses what the main characters do not deliver. From the acoustical point of view, it is somewhat akin to the calls of the Balinese kecak chant and the refrain of the frog chorus in *The Frogs* by Aristophanes.

---

[45] Cem turns up. He moves around in the garage, and occasionally tests a car by sitting in it and stepping on the gas.

[46] Metal shares many of the attributes of the element air, and for that reason breath and airy sounds are frequently traceable in the music.

[47] Isa's Hunt.

Example 25: *Die Jagd*, Scene V, "Nacht, Damals (B)," Cem-chant sequence (excerpt), b. 13–16

Example 26: *Die Jagd*, Scene V, "Nacht, Damals (B)," "Er läuft … und drückt […]" sequence (excerpt), b. 49–51

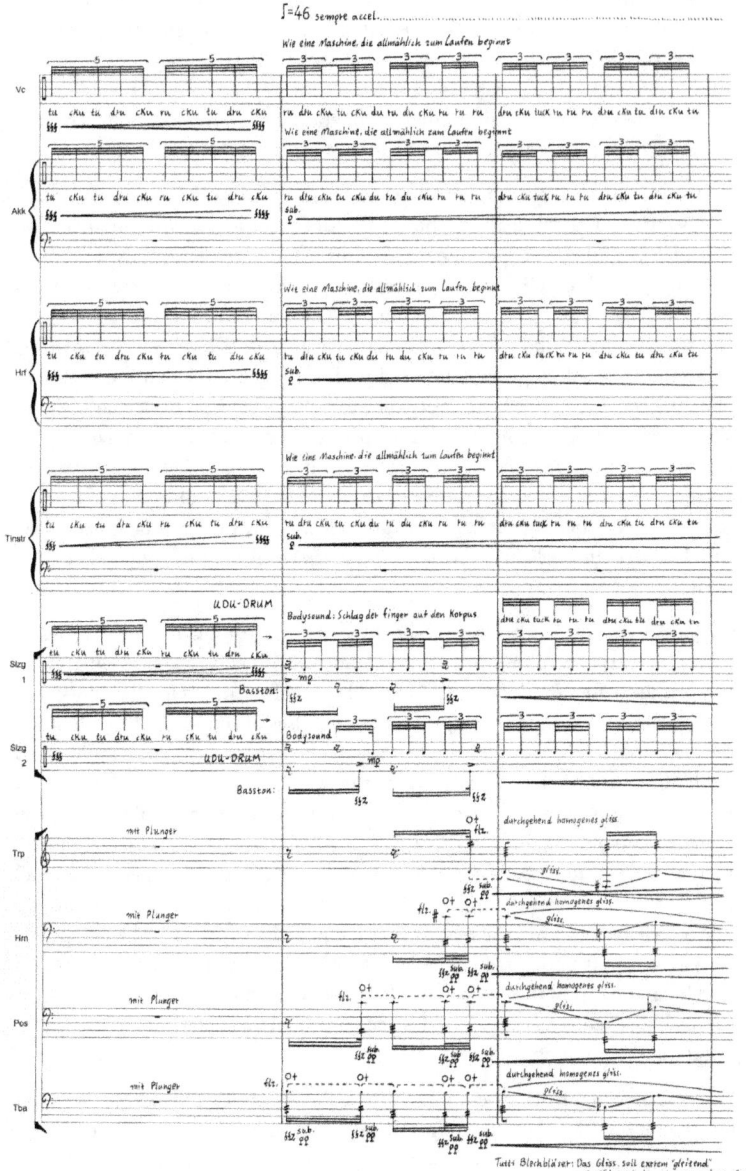

Regardless of whether the score gives utterance to vocal actions that are formulated with or without the libretto, it transmutes the semantics of the literary text – either the semantic value of isolated lexemes or the semantic interpretation of larger units – into autonomous semantics of musical creation. The sound elements are endogenously interrelated to form a coherent whole. Ergo, the vocal capability and the human phonetic practice reach a more vivid expressivity than clearly articulated words.

In everyday life, people employ an endless number of sounds, such as auditory expressions and non-lexical vocables, without semantic but with purely expressive roles: laughter, warning signals, screams of pain, anxiety vocals, suppressed yearning, and threnodial melody resembling constructs,[48] to name but a few. In particular, laughter, due to its phonetic features and conceptual interpretation, appertains to the inherent dramatic quality of *Die Jagd*. The manifold facets and types of laughter composed within the score refer to the vocal passage in Scene XIV, "Isas Jagd," between bars 298–311, a point of major significance in the opera (Example 27). This passage encloses five dissimilar laughter formations, each graphically and meticulously notated in an individual way. Textually delineated above the staff lines, nuances of expression like irony, explosiveness, laughing oneself to death, stylization, provocation, mechanization, hysteria, and delirium proclaim the diversity of the incorporated laughter modes.

Die Jagd's episode with laughter begins with a virtuosic monorhythmic sequence of Maria, a coloratura soprano, and Andy, a countertenor, on contrasting pitches, based on the sounds "Ha," "Ho," "Hu," and "He" (b. 298–304^1). The laughter is usually made up of repeated pulses of sound, as in the first bar: Ha-Ha-Ha-Ha. Nonetheless, in the following bar, the laughter morphs abruptly into an artificial commixture of the syllables in succession. Carried out by the singers Maria and Andy and the juvenile vocal ensemble, the second sequence contains rapid repetitive laughter impulses on a steady pitch level with irregularly interspersed singing-laughter outbursts on varied tone levels until b. 308. The actors Maria and Andy perform the third sequence explosively in a stylized and provocative posture; the juvenile vocal ensemble adopts the fourth one, built upon artificial laughter in sundry glissando curves. The singers Maria and Andy implement the fifth sequence mechanically, with as-fast-as-possible repetitive laughter and staccato articulation with exact rhythmical glissando directions and accentuations.

At the second sequence's penultimate bar, the laughter's polyphonic structure is superimposed by the unanticipated polyrhythmic formation of the car sex-

---

[48] A sequence of multifarious acoustic elements of mourning and expressions of grief.

tet's horns. While the horns extend their vibrant presence up to the end of the episode, Maria, Andy (both singers and actors), and the juvenile vocal ensemble gradually impose a distinctive laughter configuration. With the absence of any libretto intonation, the dramatization and dynamic reciprocity of the musicalized laughter and the car horns maximize tension and generate a sharpened sense of intensity. The episode with laughter functions as the cumulative method for reaching the plot's culmination point: Benni's scream-like singing at his highest register (G$\sharp_5$, b. 312). The instrumental insert of the car horns magnifies the laughter progression. This is a typical tactic behind my compositional modus operandi: the moment is superheated until it is energetically compelled to jump to another state in the manner of a quantum leap in particle physics. Charles Baudelaire emphasizes the double nature of the comic mode, stemming from the diabolical origins of the sense of humour. Comparatively, Cem, who personifies the double role of the car dealer and the devil/seducer, tends towards an ironic laughing attitude, as it appears by his first vocal proclamation in Scene XIV, "Isas Jagd" ("Ha – Ho – Ha," b. 163–164, 171–172). Cem's stance lies between reality and imagination. Contrary to this, Andy and Maria's viewpoints are monodirectional, circulating within the dimensional space of reality. The only family member able to recognize the forest's transformation and face Cem is Isabell.

The composition concerns the opposing standpoints of truth and falsehood, cognition and misunderstanding, humans and animals. This is supplementary to the antithetical pairs of the plot, cohesively to the boundaries between reality and imagination. Aristotle observed that only the human animal laughs, for it is cognizant of its mortality. Umberto Eco mentions that humans began laughing because they comprehend that they are mortal. Except from collecting plentiful hunted animals, and the three hunting scenes of Andy, Maria, and Isabell (IX, XII, XIV), the death is not fundamentally adduced in *Die Jagd*. The key moment of the plot occurs right before the laughter episode, at the tragic awareness of Isabell (b. 289): "Dieser Waldboden ist kein Waldboden? Aber dieses Hirschgeweih, ist unser Hirschgeweih."[49] From this moment, Cem, who just had his final solo appearance, is hermeneutically personified by the laughter succession, and, subsequently, by the climax of the city's voices at the end of the scene. Isabell's tragic consciousness crescendos immediately after the laughter episode into Benni's scream-like singing. In view of Isabell's drama, the opera reproduces the characterization of contemporary tragedy. Consequently, the tragic mood dominates the comportment of the music in the last scene XVI, "Nachlicht."[50]

---

[49] Is this forest not our forest? But this antler is our antler.

[50] Afterlight.

Example 27: *Die Jagd*, Scene XIV, "Isas Jagd," laughter episode, the five modes of laughter, b. 303–312

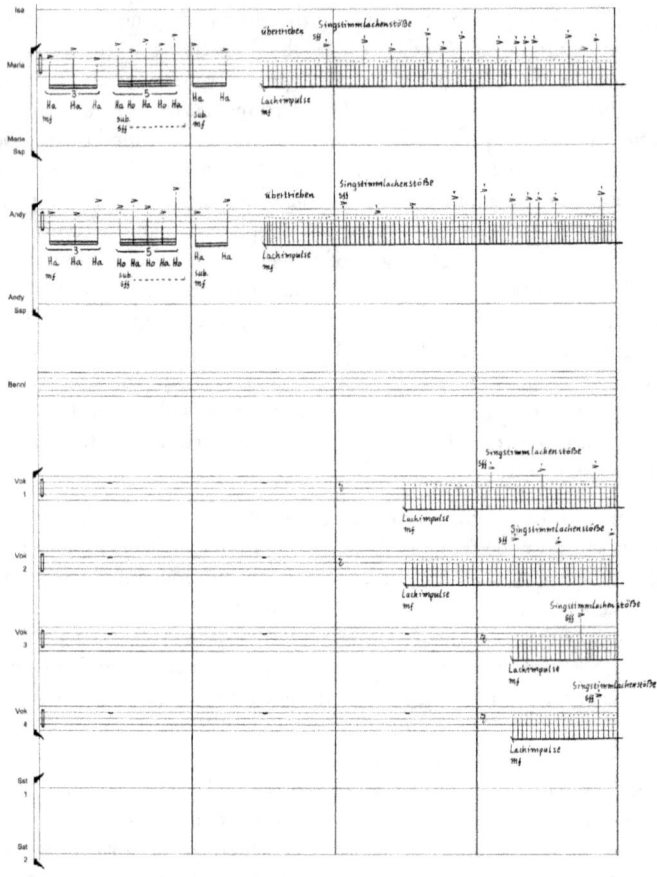

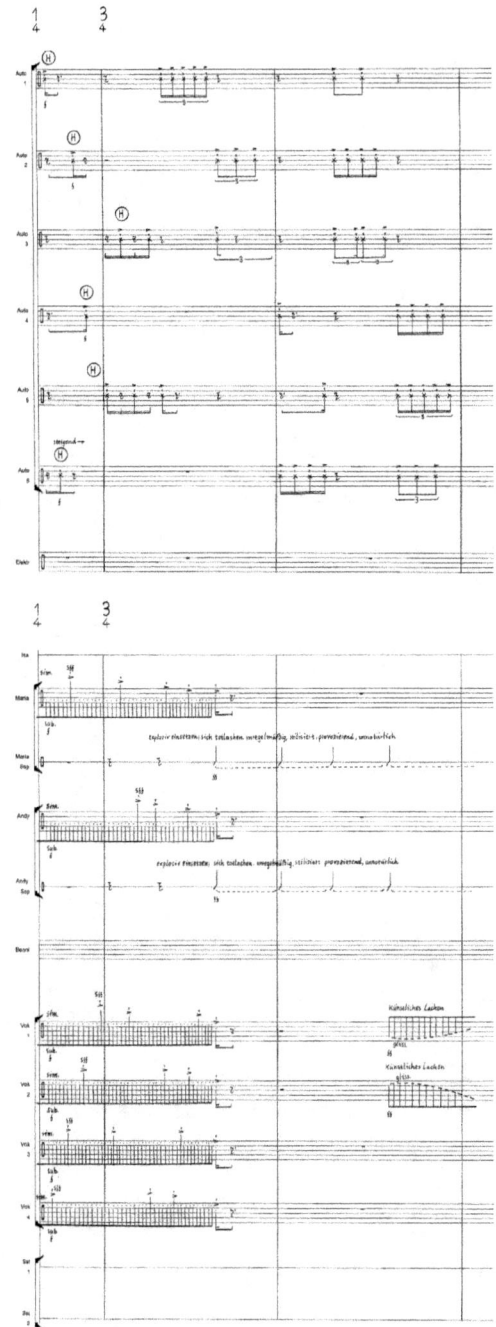

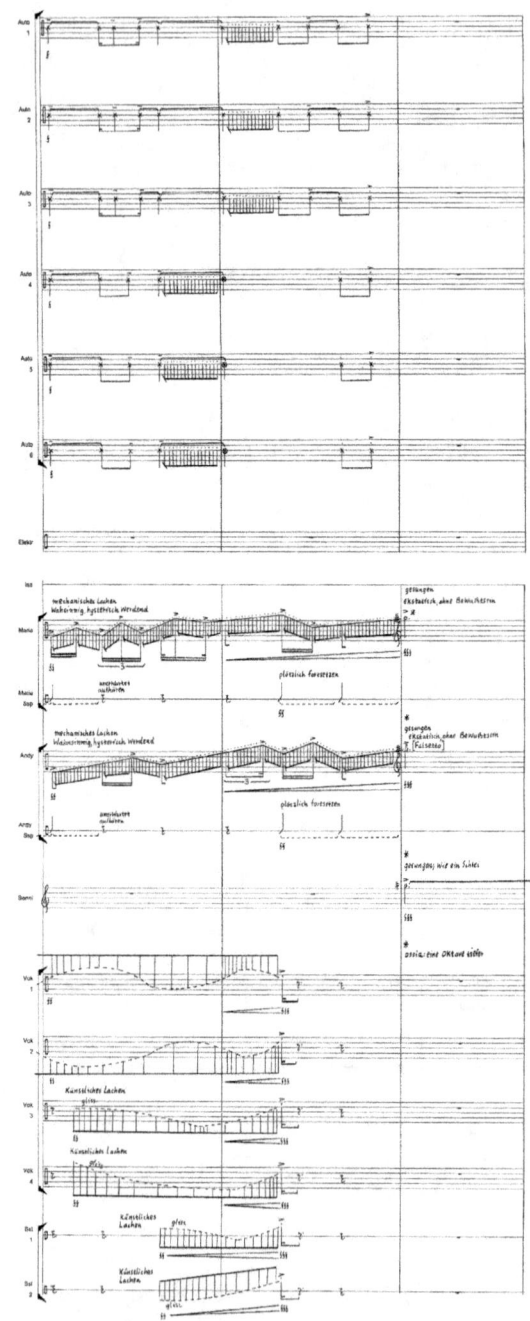

CHAPTER III

The Original Text-Related Parameters and the Consequences of Theatricality of the Music in *Akanthai* and *Die Jagd*

In a retrospective study of the aspects demonstrated in the previous chapter, the compositional processes illustrate multiple applications concerning the connection between the artistic media of music and literature. It has been evidenced that within these processes the literary elements obtain an original interpretation and implement an atypical methodology. The scope of the final chapter is to highlight three further text-related parameters of the music in conjunction with their aesthetic issues: the titles of the works, the delineated expressive nuances, as well as the descriptive commentaries and textual depictions found in the score. In addition to this, the consequences of two-dimensional theatricality and meta-theatricality will be outlined.

A title exhibits the leitmotif of the metaphorical associations or incorporates a self-pictorial and allegorical dimension. In the orchestral piece *Akanthai* (*Thorns*), according to the program notes:

> The composition is not envisioned as a requiem for Archbishop Kyprianos, but rather as a type of double-sided 'thorns dress': On one side, the thorns stand with the tips outward for defence; on the other side, the tips are directed as an attack and mortification for the body. 'Biting' and 'skewering' is regarded as an act of symbolic consequence.

However, a number of titles mirror the approximation of the production process undertaken during the synthesis development, in the sense of reflecting the composition's biographical evolution. At the same time, the title conveys the origin and quintessence of the work. Collectively with the program notes, the opus's overall aesthetic qualities are thus enriched; the perception form still retains an overt interpretational notion.

Die Jagd is subtitled "Naturoper mit Autos"[51] because of the consideration of the antithetical poles of nature and technology, reality and imagination. The opera was composed for and premiered in a unique performance space: a large two-floor car showroom. The transformation space, where the realistic dimension of the showroom metamorphoses itself into the imaginary of the forest,

---

[51] Opera for nature and cars.

emanates from the ordinary character of the car showroom. The forest stands as a symbolic motif of desire towards its own natural existence, and towards a native state that becomes lost in the conflict with the technical world. Technology is the sole portal to recapture the natural condition. In the basic sense, it materializes by way of an outing into the forest. Therewith technology itself, the technologized condition, becomes the secondary state of nature.

Besides what the title *Die Jagd* (*The Hunt*) intimates for the story, it encompasses an in total compositional strategem in two different exigencies: the sound is hunted; that is to say, the sound is interminably pursued through the individual vocal-instrumental parts. This is an implementation that involves the occurrence of the copious microstructures, based on the methodological advancement upon the proceedings of the model of permanent fleetingness. Second of all, the hunt is related to the gestural schema of linear sound wandering within the score. Identical sound impulses slide in space from one musician to the next, as eventuates in "Nacht, Damals (A)" with the words "auf null gefahren"[52] and "Reset" of the juvenile vocal ensemble (b. 20–23). Space rotations and sound circulations emerge with varied complexity.

The aspect of permanent mobility (see 2.1.5.) finds de novo application and becomes effective by the plenitude of subtle expressive nuances that are textually implemented in both vocal and instrumental sections. Additional to the standard parameters of musical notation, at narrowest distance and often within a polyphonic or homophonic structure, these uncommon textual indications are provided identically as well as divergently. For example, observing Scene VIII of *Die Jagd*, "Walden,"[53] the modulation of Andy's singing sequence changes in bars 46–55 and follows the association fields of ironic and mocking → irritation → with inner anger → dolce → delirium → hysteria → delirium → accusing (Example 28). In a manner pertinent to serial thinking, a broad palette of sound colour differentiations and expressive gradations is instigated. In this context, mobility turns out to be variably advantageous: as a certain negation of clear contours, it imparts an anti-naturalistic quality and suggests an expressive mood direction that is always construed differently. It also aims at stimulant reinforcement and dramatic increase of the performer's interpretation that inevitably evokes theatricality.

Textual depictions are not to be understood as illustrative or programmatically binding. On the contrary, associative leeway is given to affect fine acoustic differentiations. They pursue a conceivable description of certain sound qualities that are impossible to be notated by solely traditional means of notation.

---

[52] Driven to zero.

[53] Life in the Woods.

Next to the familiar and basic musical colouration, there occurs a new and supplementary coalescence. For example:

i. The singers depict instructions such as "martially, like a rifle" ("Walden," b. 104–105), or in a self-multi-voiced approach analogous to multiphonics (b. 80–82);

ii. The instrumentalists transmit verbal specifications such as birdlike sonorities with the cello, accordion, harp, and celesta ("Geräusche," b. 42–43), bubbles with the trombone and tuba (b. 38), a car horn ("Isas Jagd," b. 61) and a large pendulum ("Nacht, Damals [A]," b. 43–55) with the brass quartet.

The articulation of textual depictions and expressive nuances are collateral to the fundamental auditory attributes of sound. This adds an additional degree of complexity; providing an enriched image of notation does not, however, connote complication. The score is not a directory of sound atoms, signs, textual instructions, and explanations. On the contrary, it establishes the possibility to mutably combine and integrate a variety of basic notational parameters. Moreover, it focuses upon active synthesis, fluent transitional transformation, multifaceted shadings, and fields of convergence and divergence. The composite soundfields serve the clarification of construction, but also benefit from ambiguity.

Because of the dramatic property of the specified expressive nuances, it is not a histrionic situation that is sounding; it is the constructed sound structure that becomes theatrical. The theatrical element is not parallel to the sound, but rather emerges from the sound as a new layer, a profound component of the music. The inherent theatricality is conveyed by the articulation of the sound that happens in the brains of the musicians, in the vertiginous interplay between dream, memory, alertness, and trauma. The theatrical gesture is formed by the collision of different inner processes and different states of consciousness that tangentially alternate. Depending upon the interpretation, these inner processes turn inside out. Interior and exterior, audible and inaudible, visible and invisible, sound and silence intercede, as they are not opposites. Furthermore, especially for opera singers, the scenic parameter profits from a two-dimensional theatricality, one that is inborn in the music referring to the work-immanent compositional polymediality, and another that accrues out of the staged conception corresponding to this polymediality on the plane of staging.

Generally speaking, the sound complexes possess a self-constructed gestural plasticity and an eloquence of narration. They suggest an inwardly expanded, meta-theatrical, and invisible acoustic space. In so doing, a double fictional corollary concurrently comes to light. One is related to the libretto and the staged events, and the other is utterly adduced by the music's deportment.

Reminiscent of ancient Greek tragedy, the play does not offer a real struggle on stage; the struggle manifests offstage. In a comparable manner, the music prevents any direct, obvious rendering of the literary source. In actuality, it signifies the interaction and confrontation between the two media. The poem's and libretto's elements are thereby an integral component of the musical synthesis by which they are represented. As in *Akanthai*, the piece exclusively scored for instrumentalists with acoustically oriented figurative processes, includes vocal insertions. This particular procedure aims to supplant Aristotelian mimesis, the idea of imitating an action, evoking a quasi-imitation of the text. The composition, as an acoustical self-reflection of the literary source, constructs a clustered network of musical topoi, thus revealing a complex intertwining of meta- and connotative-layers.

Example 28: *Die Jagd*, Scene VIII, "Walden," b. 46–55

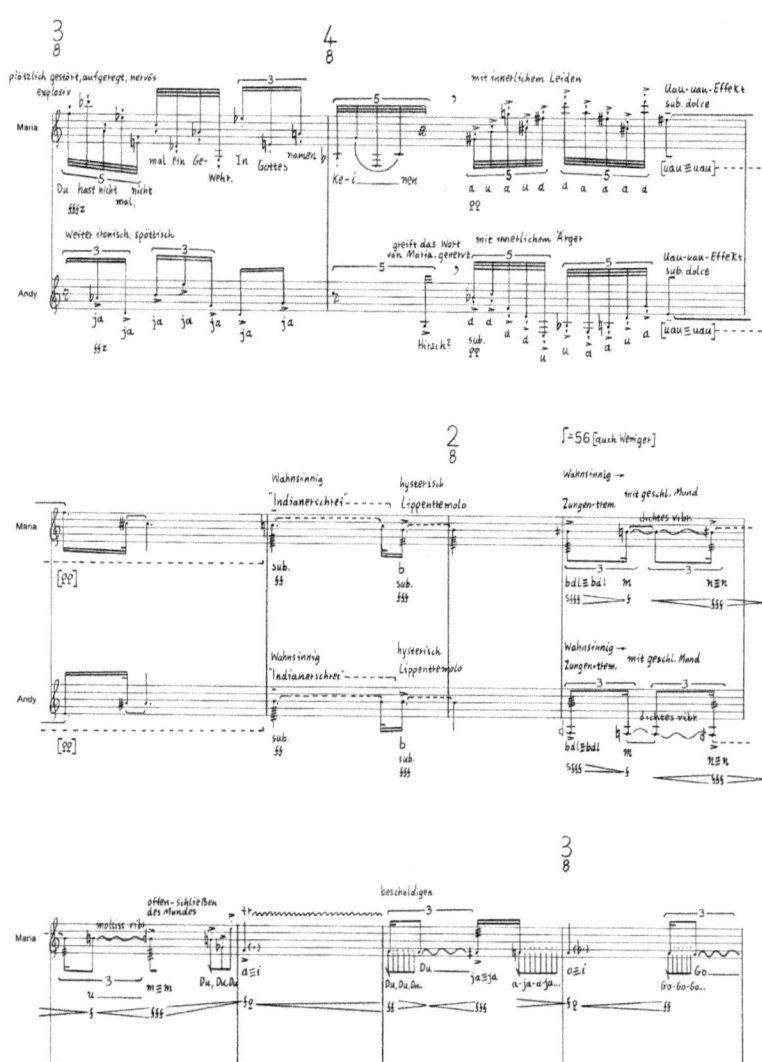

89

APPENDIX I

Polymediality, Percussivity, and Hybridity

In 2002, my first musico-theatrical composition *My Eyes, Only You* for two actors was premiered at the Vienna Concert Hall of the Mozarteum Foundation in Salzburg. Since then, the inclusion of extra-musical elements at the forefront of creative processes has played a critical role in the development of the concept of polymediality.

I began to be interested in music perception and cognition by attempting interdisciplinary approaches to existing pieces, thus employing multimedia staging for the performance of vocal and instrumental works. This resulted in the production of a concert trilogy: the staged concerts *Burning Motions* for seven actors and instrumental ensemble,[54] *Refurbished* for 18 musicians,[55] and *Das Geheimnis des Kleiderbügels*[56] for five actors and 22 musicians.[57] A year later, *Hydor Chronos*, for electroacoustic music and video, was performed at the Salzburg Easter Festival.

With the composition *Strophes* for choir, instrumental ensemble, loudspeaker ensemble and electronics, exclusively written for the Volkswagen Transparent Factory in Dresden (2003–04), I have introduced a new component into the music that has become essential in my practice: composing for unusual performance spaces. Taking music outside of opera houses and concert halls instigated a number of other polymedial works, such as the opera *As Time Goes By*, premiered by the Hanover State Opera in the eight-storey building of the Ministry of Science and Culture of Lower Saxony (2005), the media opera *Die Reise des G. Mastorna*[58], performed at the Salzburg Airport (Amadeus Terminal 2) within the frame of the Mozart Festival 2006, the vocal piece *Aquanauten*, premiered in the gardens of the Mirabell Palace in Salzburg (2007), and the opera *Die Jagd*, premiered by the Stuttgart State Opera in a large car showroom (2008).

From an antithetical viewpoint, unconventional instruments are positioned on the stage of classical concert halls. In the case of *Autotrio*, a composition for three cars, fourteen car-musicians and electronics (2010), the premiere took place in the 2,300-seat Rosengarten Mozart Hall in Mannheim.

---

[54] Premiered at the Vienna Concert Hall in Salzburg, 2004.
[55] Premiered at the Central State Theatre Salzburg, 2005.
[56] The Secret of the Hanger.
[57] Premiered at the Toihaus Theatre Salzburg, 2005.
[58] The Journey of G. Mastorna.

For the finale of the celebrations of the 125th birthday of the automobile, I was commissioned by the City of Mannheim and the Agentur m:con-mannheim:congress GmbH to write the open-air multimedia symphony *Autosymphonic* (2010–11). The one-hour symphony is scored for large orchestra, choir, children's choir, pop band vocal ensemble, 80 automobiles, 120 automobile players (percussionists), percussion octet, live electronics and a 360-degree sound system. After a ten-month casting whereby the sound possibilities of every car were extensively explored (Example 29), I created a car orchestra consisting of 80 automobiles of various types and eras. The symphony employs circa 800 car sounds (Example 30). The premiere took place at the main square of Mannheim, the Friedrichsplatz, and required 290 musicians (SWR Baden-Baden and Freiburg Symphony Orchestra, SWR Vocal Ensemble Stuttgart, Stuttgart State Opera Children's Chorus), 17 conductors (three main and 14 secondary), 75 technicians and 400 loudspeakers. It attracted an audience of 20,000 people. Horst Hamann designed scenery consisting of lasers, lights, videos, urban screenings, and 3-D projection mapping synchronized to the music.

The mediation between so-called classical and popular music gains increasing importance in my recent works, in terms of practical, aesthetic, and, not least, social issues. In *Autosymphonic*, for example, 120 adolescents performed the 80 cars. They were selected in castings and trained for a year by the University of Popular Music Baden-Württemberg. In addition, Part IV of the same piece, *Der Traum*,[59] is composed for symphony orchestra, choir, and the singers and rappers of the pop band Söhne Mannheims. Soul artist Xavier Naidoo sang the solo vocals.

Composing music for cultural events, for large audiences from different cultural backgrounds, is both a challenge and an opportunity. The challenge is to bring together high culture and a contemporary event in a dynamic tension. With the integration of familiar and everyday objects into a new context, the opportunity lies in the definition of the term cultural event as an innovative and future-oriented artistic form.

For specific works, the employment of electronic media and advanced technology obtains a great role in the process of composition and realization. For example, the production of *Vertumnus* for electronic music, loudspeaker orchestra and three-dimensional interactive shadow puppetry, premiered on the big stage of the Macedonian Opera and Ballet in Skopje (2009). In *Autosymphonic*, the whole Friedrichsplatz was transformed into a concert stage area of

---

[59] The Dream.

65,000 square meters with 13 stages placed around the square.[60] In order to enable the projection of sounds at the positions where the musicians were located, a 360-degree sound system in 14.1 surround format was installed. Sophisticated hardware and software equipment supported the work's performance, including Matrix3, a multichannel digital audio mixing and processing system, and D-Mitri, a Gigabit network-based digital audio processing and distribution platform.

---

[60] In one semicircle the car orchestra; positioned opposite, the orchestra, choir and the four percussion stages.

Example 29: *Autosymphonic*, car casting, sound library overview, p. 1

	Motor	Horn	Door[1]	Door[2]	Buttons/ Switches/ Clicks	Indicator	Windows	Boot[2] Motor Lungs	Handbrake	Tank	Wheels/ Spikes	Gears	Strokes	Rimbed	Sandpaper	Tremols	Ventilation Rotary Controller	Various
LUXURY																		
Rolls Royce Silver Cloud		+(20)	+					+/-					1. Ashtray (3) 2. Gearstick (7) 3. Armrest (9) 4. Oil dipstick (11)					Motor start with removed ignition cable (1, 2)
Rolls Royce Silver Shadow		+(11)	+		1. Door Handle (3) 2. Door Closer (4) 3. Central Locking (6) 4. Map/Window Switches (16)			+/-		-(2 Pers.) (7)			1. Spring (Feeler) of Motor (10) Boot/Screwdrivers (9) 2. Glove Box (12) 3. Ashtray (13)					1. Cooler Handle Pull/Release (10) 2. Ventilation Lever (14) 3. High Beam lever - Ventilation Switch Pull/Release (15)
MB S600 W100	+	+(8)	+		+(10)			+/-										Deflation: Ableness (11)
EXECUTIVE																		
MB W108		+(9)	+		1. Radio keys (3) 2. Luggs. Boot Handle (7) 3. Ventilation Clap of the Door (11)			+ with deflect springs) (5)+					Glove Box (5)			Motor Grill		1. Squared/Electric (3) 2. Co-Drivers Seat (6) 3. Ventilation and Temperature levers (10)
MB 280 SEL					1. Lock/Motor Boot (7) 2. Switch/Damper (8) 3. Lock Luggs. Boot (10)	+(9)		+/- (14)					1. Glove Box (10) 2. Bag Set 3. Belt (12) 4. Armrest/Hand (11) -3 between Kontick-holes Boot-Body/Plastic flint (15) 6. Ventilation Lovers between Motor Boot Plate/Plastic Rod (17) 7. Motor Cover/2 Metal Rods (19) 8. Cover of Oil Overflow/Metal Key (20) 9. Cover of Oil Overflow/Metal Rod (21)	Radiator Grill/Plastic Rod (4)	Ashtray (9)	1. Motor Grill/Metal Rod (3) 2. Motor Grill/Plastic Rod (15)	+(11)	1. Antenna Pull(-n)/Damped with Hand. To Stopped with plastic Rod 2. Cooler/Metal Roll: Ventilation Wheel sounds like a Bell (18)
COMPACT																		
MB 200 Diesel	1. Half Motor Start (1) 2. Motor Start Tenth. (2)	+(14)			1. Empty Boot/Clapper (3) 2. Lights Switch (15) 3. Door Locker (17) 4. Closure (Vorschluss) M over Boot (20)		1. +(4) 2. Opens/Clo se with Crank (18)	-(19)		-(4)			1. Belt Pulled (6) 2. Belt Holding Lower Part (7) 3. Glove Box (8) 4. Armrest Cover (12) 5. Antennas (21)		Ashtray (9)	Motor Grill	+(11)	1. Ashtray/Glove Box Combination (10) 2. Seat Lever Pull/Release (13) 3. Wiper (without water) (16)

[1] With/without pulled handle close/open
[2] With/without pulled handle close/open

Example 30: *Autosymphonic*, "IX. Finale" for 12 solo automobiles, automobile orchestra in nine groups, symphony orchestra and choir, p. 139, b. 1–11

IX.

FINALE

**for 12 solo automobiles, automobile orchestra in 9 groups, 120 automobile players,
symphony orchestra, choir, children's choir, pop band vocal ensemble,
percussion octet and electronics**

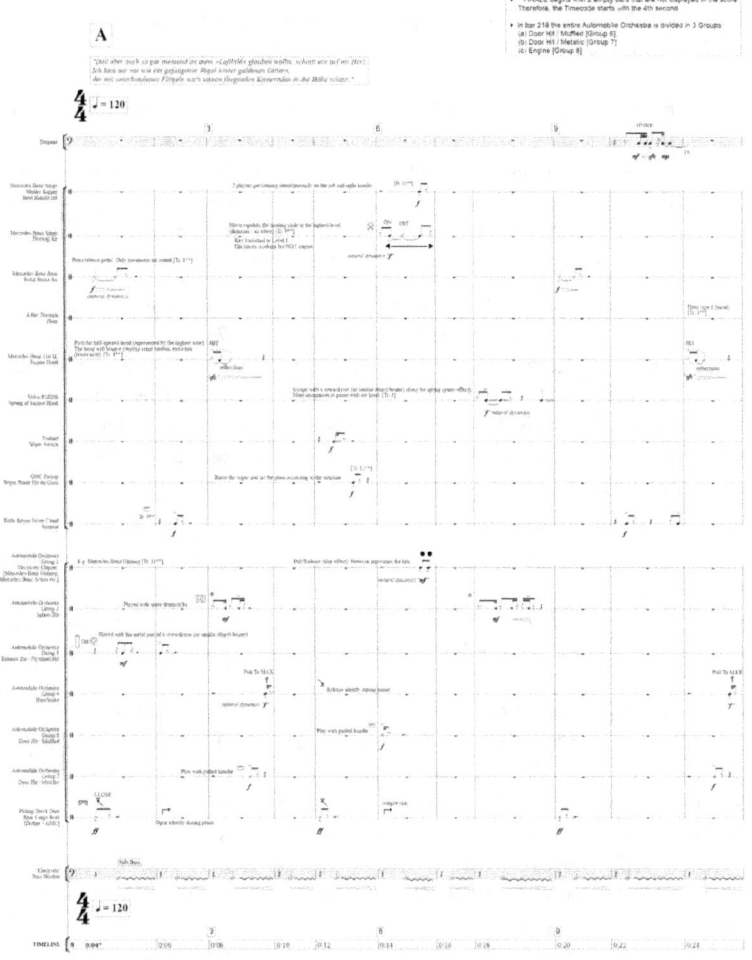

A quintessential focal point of my music concerns approaching instruments in a percussive manner. This was initially applied in *Staubzucker* for guitar quartet in 2007.[61] The particular processing is of fundamental importance especially when composing for unconventional apparatuses, as in the case of the car sextet in the opera *Die Jagd* and the car orchestra in *Autosymphonic*. The cars are played like percussion instruments. Similarly, most of the choral parts in *Humans and Machines*, part III of *Autosymphonic*, are composed in a percussive-mechanical way (Example 31).

Another central concern involves hybridity, not in terms of a musical amalgam, genre-like, but referring to original practices that comprise a diverse spectrum of hybridization processes. Some classification models of hybridity are:

i. Hybrid instrumentation between atypical instruments and voices with the enclosure of incongruous sound apparatuses (e.g. in *C Story*, *Akanthai*, and *Die Jagd*). In this context, to see heterogeneity not as the source of conflict, but as the promising condition for compositional practices, hybridity intervenes to enunciate a third-space acoustic identity, change its value and criteria of recognition;

ii. Hybrid rendering in *En Plo*, for contrabass clarinet, double bass, electronic sounds and loudspeaker orchestra (2007), five electroacoustic transducer groups of different kinds and types, distributed in space, provoke the projection of a timbre-mixed sonic character, whereas, in *Cursed*, for guitar solo or for classical and electric guitar duet (2009), only a single tone, E, is used ten times, on all possible positions on the fingerboard;

iii. Hybrid circulation is a cycle in which an existing mosaic structure or a mini hybridized particle is exploited in a new context, or serves to generate another hybrid assemblage; comparably, mixed structures of an instrumental/vocal work are compiled into a new framework in another piece (*Holy Bread*, *Akanthai*, *Autosymphonic*).

A number of works, like *C Story* and *Whiteblack*, were composed as a response to the 1974 Turkish invasion of Cyprus, the cataclysmic event in contemporary Cypriot history. Of concern here are not the ethnic issues, but an attempt to exorcise the tragedy and, moreover, a general humanistic and antiwar commitment. The same qualities appear in the simplistic epigrammatic poems of Costas Montis whose verses are traceable in my music. A central meaning possesses the application of textual elements and vocality in instrumental works,

---

[61] The same piece exists in a version for amplified Paetzold recorder trio or quartet (2010).

like in *Holy Bread*, with the subtitle "Requiem for Costas Montis," for amplified string quartet (2004), *Elpis* for accordion orchestra (2006–07), *Thalatta, Thalatta!* for mandolin and ensemble (2007), and *Akanthai* for large orchestra (2009).

The characteristic that often influences the critical perspective is achieved by the interjection of allegorical humorous elements. Influenced by the ancient Greek comedies and the idiom of the Greek-Cypriot dialect, the aspect of humour is particularly present in the vocal pieces, as in *Tempus Tantum Nostrum Est* for vocal ensemble and motorcycles (2005).

Example 31: *Autosymphonic*, "III. Humans and Machines," for choir and symphony orchestra, p. 53, b. 41–53

APPENDIX II

References

1. Bibliography

Aitken, Hugh. *The Piece as a Whole: Studies in Holistic Musical Analysis.* Westport, CT: Greenwood Press, 1997.

Anoyanakis, Fivos and Alekos Iakovides, eds. *Cyprus Popular Music.* Text and audio CDs. Nafplion: Peloponnesian Folklore Foundation, 1999.

Aristotle. *De Anima,* with introduction and commentary by Sir David Ross. Oxford: Clarendon Press, 1961.

– *Poetics,* transl. with an introduction and notes by Malcolm Heath. London: Penguin Classics, 1996.

– *The Art of Rhetoric,* transl. by Hugh Lawson-Tancred. London: Penguin Classics, 1991.

"Art also requires courage – High Culture as a People's Event: The Autosymphonic." In *m:convisions.* 11, 10–11. Mannheim: m:con, 2011.

Bachmann, Ingeborg. *Die Hörspiele: Ein Geschäft mit Träumen, Die Zikaden, Der Gute Gott von Manhattan.* Munich: Piper, 1996.

Barber, Cesar Lombardi. *Shakespeare's Festive Comedy: A Study of Dramatic Form and its Relation to Social Custom.* Princeton: Princeton University Press, 1959.

Barthes, Roland. *Image, Music, Text,* transl. by Stephen Heath. Hammersmith, London: Fontana Press, 1977.

Bauer, Karin. *Adorno's Nietzschean Narratives: Critiques of Ideology, Readings of Wagner.* New York: State University of New York Press, 1999.

Bennett, Tony, Colin Mercer and Jane Woollacott, eds. *Popular Culture and Social Relations.* Milton Keynes: Open University Press, 1986.

Beyer, Hermann and Siegfried Mauser, eds. *Zeitphilosophie und Klanggestalt: Untersuchungen zum Werk Bernd Alois Zimmermanns.* Mainz: Schott, 1986.

Braun, Michael. *Hörreste, Sehreste: Das Literarische Fragment bei Büchner, Kafka, Benn und Celan.* Cologne: Böhlau, 2002.

Brecht, Bertold. *Schriften zum Theater*. Frankfurt: Suhrkamp, 1999.

Bruhn, Siglind, ed. *Sonic Transformations of Literary Texts: From Program Music to Musical Ekphrasis*. Hillsdale, NY: Pendragon Press, 2008.

Colvin, Stephen. *Dialect in Aristophanes: The Politics of Language in Ancient Greek Literature*. Oxford: Oxford University Press, 1999.

Cox, Christoph and Daniel Warner, eds. *Audio Culture: Readings in Modern Music*. New York: Continuum, 2004.

Cuddon, J. A., *A Dictionary of Literary Terms and Literary Theory*, revised by M.A.R. Habib. 5th ed. Oxford: Wiley-Blackwell, 2013.

Danuser, Hermann. "On Postmodernism in Music." In *International Postmodernism: Theory and Literary Practice*, vol. XI, edited by Hans Bertens and Douwe Fokkema, 157–166. Amsterdam and Philadelphia: John Benjamins, 1997.

Dunsby, Jonathan. *Making Words Sing: Nineteenth- and Twentieth-Century Song*. Cambridge: Cambridge University Press, 2004.

Eastmond, Antony and Liz James, eds. *Icon and Word: The power of Images in Byzantium*. Aldershot: Ashgate, 2003.

Ebbeke, Klaus. *Zeitschichtung: Gesammelte Aufsätze zum Werk von Bernd Alois Zimmermann*. Mainz: Schott, 1998.

Eco, Umberto. *The Limits of Interpretation*. Bloomington: Indiana University Press, 1990.

Eddie, William Alexander. *Charles Valentin Alkan: His Life and his Music*. Burlington: Ashgate, 2007.

Elia, Marios Joannou. *Die Jagd: Naturoper mit Autos*. Programme booklet. Stuttgart: Staatsoper, 2008.

- "Polymedialität als Konzept – Die Multimediasinfonie autosymphonic." In *Ästhetik des Vorläufigen: Skizze – Entwurf – Probe*. edited by Thomas Hochradner, Reihe Wissenschaft und Kunst, 189–196. Heidelberg: Universitätsverlag Winter, 2014.

- "Polymedialität als Konzept." In *Autosymphonic*, edited by Horst Hamann, 27–39. Mannheim: Edition Quadrat, 2012.

- *Zeitgenössische Musik im Kontext von Polyästhetik und Polymedialität*. Mainz: Schott Music, 2016 [urn:nbn:de:101:1-201609303630].

Godøy, Rolf Inge and Marc Leman, eds. *Musical Gestures: Sound, Movement and Meaning.* New York: Routledge, 2010.

Grafen, Joachim. "Der starke Sang des leichten Motors." In *autosymphonic.* Programme book, 21–31. Mannheim: m:con, 2011.

Grund, Vera. "Between Freedom and Determination: Marios Joannou Elia's Music for Guitar." In *Perspectives of New Music*, vol. 53, no. 2. edited by Benjamin Boretz, Robert Morris, and John Rahn, 177–188. Seattle, 2015.

Hamann, Horst, ed. *Autosymphonic.* Mannheim: Edition Quadrat, 2012.

Hedling, Erik and Ulla-Britta Lagerroth, eds. *Cultural Functions of Intermedial Exploration.* Amsterdam and New York: Rodopi, 2002.

Hiekel, Jörn Peter. "Die Sprechaktionen im vierten Satz der *Antiphonen*." In *Bernd Alois Zimmermanns Requiem für einen jungen Dichter.* Beihefte zum Archiv für Musikwissenschaft, vol. XXXVI, 45–61. Stuttgart: Franz Steiner, 1995.

"Humans and Machines: An Interview with Composer Marios Joannou Elia at the Royal Festival Hall in London." In *Zeitschichten.* Interview with Paul Michael Coleman, University of Westminster, December 24, 2010, accessed March 15, 2011, http://www.zeitschichten.com/2010/12/24/elia.

Kagel, Mauricio. *Anagrama.* London: Universal Edition, 1965.

Kapre-Karka, K. *Love and the Symbolic Journey in the Poetry of Cavafy, Eliot, and Seferis: An Interpretation with Detailed Poem-By-Poem Analysis.* New York: Pella, 1982.

Kerman, Joseph. *Opera as Drama.* Berkeley and Los Angeles: University of California Press, 2005.

Kitto, H. D. F. "The Chorus" in *Greek Tragedy: A Literary Study*, 158–170. Oxford: Routledge, 2003.

Kling, Susanne. "Marios Joannou Elia: Polymedialität als Konzept. Musik im Dialog mit aussermusikalischen Medien." In *autosymphonic.* Programme book, 32–33. Mannheim: m:con, 2011.

Komponist Marios Joannou Elia im Gespräch mit Dramaturg Xavier Zuber über die Zeitoper "Schwabengarage – Die Jagd". Stuttgart: Journal des Staatstheaters Stuttgart, December 2008.

Kraml, Peter. *(Marios Joannou) Elia – Genauso wie die Ilias. An den Klippen der Küste. Erinnerungsfüllsel. Erkrankung als Entzauberung versus Entzauberung als Erkrankung.* ORF Radio, unpublished manuscript, 2008.

– *Marios Joannou Elia: Warum Staubzucker, das Gegenteil und der Vorteil.* ORF Radio, unpublished manuscript, 2008.

Kunkel, Michael and Martina Papiro, eds. *Der Schall: Mauricio Kagels Instrumentarium.* Saarbrücken: Pfau 2009.

Le Goff, Jacques. *The Medieval Imagination.* translated by Arthur Goldhammer. Chicago: University of Chicago Press, 1988.

Leighton, Hodson, ed. *Marcel Proust: The Critical Heritage.* London and New York: Routledge, 1989.

Ley, Graham. *A Short Introduction to the Ancient Greek Theater.* Chicago: University of Chicago Press, 1991.

Lücke, Hendrik. *Mallarmé – Debussy: Eine Vergleichende Studie zur Kunstanschauung am Beispiel von L'Après-midi d'un Faune.* Studien zur Musikwissenschaft, vol. IV. Hamburg: Dr. Kovac, 2005.

Maehder, Jürgen. "Funktionen der Sprechstimme im Experimentellen Musiktheater Mauricio Kagels." In *Stimmen – Klänge – Töne: Synergien im Szenischen Spiel.* 209–228. edited by Hans-Peter Bayerdörfer. Forum Modernes Theater, vol. XXX. Tübingen: Gunter Narr, 2002.

Makhairas, Leontios. *Recital Concerning the Sweet Land of Cyprus, Entitled "Chronicle".* edited and translated by N. M. Dawkins. 2 vols. Oxford: Clarendon Press, 1932.

McLean, Mervyn. *Maori Music.* Auckland: Auckland University Press, 1996.

Melberg, Arne. *Theories of Mimesis.* Cambridge: Cambridge University Press, 1995.

Michaelides, Vasilis. *The 9th of July 1821 in Cyprus: Drama in Greek-Cypriot Dialect.* introduction by Kyriakos Hadjioannou. Famagusta: Library of the Famagusta Greek Gymnasium, 1960.

Middleton, Richard. *Studying Popular Music.* Milton Keynes and Philadelphia: Open University Press, 1990.

Montis, Costas. *Complete Works.* Nicosia: Leventis Foundation, 1987.

– *Complete Works: Abbendum.* vols. 1–7. Nicosia: Leventis, 1988–2002.

Nietzsche, Friedrich Wilhelm. *The Birth of Tragedy and Other Writings*. Cambridge Texts in the History of Philosophy, edited by Raymond Geuss and Ronald Speirs. New York: Cambridge University Press, 1999.

Parker, Roger. *Remaking the Song: Operatic Visions and Revisions from Handel to Berio*. Berkeley: University of California Press, 2006.

Pervolarakis, Georgios. *Staubzucker by Marios Joannou Elia: a chronicle of Staubzucker by the members of the Miscelanea Guitar Quartet, reviews, the significance of the piece for the classical guitar literature*. M. A. thesis. Universität Mozarteum Salzburg, 2014.

Petruschka, Gudrun. *Marios Joannou Elia – Ein Komponistenporträt*. M. A. thesis. Hochschule für Musik und Theater München, 2007.

Randel, Don Michael, ed. *The Harvard Dictionary of Music*. 4th ed. Cambridge: Harvard University Press, 2003.

Roads, Curtis. *Microsound*. Cambridge: MIT Press, 2004.

Rosand, Ellen. *Opera in Seventeenth-Century Venice: The Creation of a Genre*. Berkeley and Los Angeles: University of California Press, 1991.

Roscher, Wolfgang. *Musik, Kunst, Kultur als Abenteuer*. Kassel: Bärenreiter, 1994.

Rubin, Leon and I. Nyoman Sedana. *Performance in Bali*. London: Routledge, 2007.

Salzman, Eric and Thomas Dézsy. *The New Music Theater: Seeing the Voice, Hearing the Body*. Oxford and New York: Oxford University Press, 2008.

Schoon, Andi. "Geräusch als Spektakel. Zu den plurimedialen Kompositionen von Marios Joannou Elia." In *Neue Zeitschrift für Musik*, 56–59. Mainz: Schott Music, 2014.

Schröter, Jens. *Intermedialität: Facetten und Probleme eines Aktuellen Medienwissenschaftlichen Begriffs*. montage/av, issue 7, no. 2, 1998, 129–154.

Schwarzbauer, Michaela. "Aqaunauten und Staubzucker – eine Hommage an Wolfgang Roscher von Marios Joannou Elia." In *25 Jahre Internationale Gesellschaft für Polyästhetische Erziehung. Erfahrungen und Perspektiven*. edited by Gerhard Hofbauer and Michaela Schwarzbauer. 207–208. Munich: Musikverlag Bernd Katzbichler, 2013.

Shulstad, Reeves. "Liszt's Symphonic Poems and Symphonies." In *The Cambridge Companion to Liszt*. edited by Kenneth Hamilton. 206–212. Cambridge and New York: Cambridge University Press, 2005.

Silk, M. S. *Aristophanes and the Definition of Comedy*. Oxford: Oxford University Press, 2000.

Sloterdijk, Peter. *Der ästhetische Imperativ*. Hamburg: Philo & Philo Fine Arts, 2007.

Smith, Helaine L. *Masterpieces of Classic Greek Drama*. Westport: Greenwood Publishing Group, 2006.

Spiegel, John. *Dimensions of Laughter in Crime and Punishment*. Selingsgrove: Susquehanna University Press, 2000.

Sternberg, Robert J. and Karin Sternberg. *Cognitive Psychology*. 7th ed. Boston, MA: Cengage/Wadsworth, 2016.

Takashi, Sugiyama. "Herder's Theory of Common Sense: The Birth of the Concept of Synesthesia." In *Aesthetics*, no. 13. Japanese Society for Aesthetics, accessed February 15, 2010, http://www.bigakukai.jp/aesthetics_online/aesthetics_13/text/text13_sugiyama.pdf.

"To widen the spectrum of possibilities." In *Zeitschichten*. Marios Joannou Elia in an interview with Matthias Roeder, Harvard University, February 8, 2009, accessed March 21, 2011, http://www.zeitschichten.com/2009/02/08/marios-joannou-elia.

Tzimurta, Giorgio. "Marios Joannou Elia – Water Stories. Das Element des Schicksals." In *Zyprischer Frühling*. Programme book. 12–13. Berlin: Kulturabteilung der Botschaft der Republik Zypern, 2010.

Varella, Stavroula. *Language Contact and the Lexicon in the History of Cypriot Greek*. Bern: Peter Lang, 2006.

"VERTUMNUS at the Biennale of Young Creators." In *Cyprus Today*. XLVII, no. 3. July – September. 58–60. Nicosia: Ministry of Education and Culture, 2009.

Wagner, Meike and Wolf-Deter Erbst, eds. *Performing the Matrix: Mediating Cultural Performances*. Munich: Epodium, 2008.

Weismüller, Christoph R. *Musik, Traum und Medien: Philosophie des Musikdramatischen Gesamtkunstwerks: Ein Medienphilosophischer Beitrag zu Richard Wagners Öffentlicher Traumarbeit*. Würzburg: Königshausen und Neumann, 2001.

Welsch, Wolfgang. *Aisthesis: Grundzüge und Perspektiven der Aristotelischen Sinneslehre*. Stuttgart: Klett-Cotta, 1987.

– *Grenzgänge der Ästhetik*. Stuttgart: Reclam, 1996.

Wolf, Werner. "Musico-Literary Intermediality and the Musicalization of Literature/Fiction: Definition and Topology." In *Musicalization of Fiction: A Study in the Theory and History of Intermediality*. 51–70. Amsterdam and Atlanta, GA: Rodopi, 1999.

Xenophon. *The Anabasis of Cyrus*. translated by Wayne Ambler, introduction by Eric Buzzetti. Ithaca and New York: Cornell University Press, 2008.

Zimmermann, Bernd Alois. *Antiphonen for viola and 25 instrumentalists*. Munich: Edition Modern, 1962.

– *Intervall und Zeit: Aufsätze und Schriften zum Werk*. Mainz: Schott, 1974.

2. Recordings

Aristophanes. *Birds*, v. 227–262. Read in the restored pronunciation of classical Greek by Stephen G. Daitz. City University of New York. The Society for the Oral Reading of Greek and Latin Literature, accessed March 13, 2011, http://www.rhapsodes.fll.vt.edu/Aristophanes/aristophanes.htm.

Baraka: A World Beyond Words. directed by Ron Fricke. DVD. MPI, 2008.

Cyprus: The Tradition. Andreas Aristidou and Kyriacos Zittis. CD. Playa Sound, 2005.

Die Mannheimer Autosinfonie – Entstehung eines Multimedia-Events. Documentary film, directed by Ursula Schwedler. SWR, 2011.

Elia, Marios Joannou. "Aquanauten – Skylla und Charybdis" and "Staubzucker." In *25 Jahre Internationale Gesellschaft für Polyästhetische Erziehung*, edited by Gerhard Hofbauer and Michaela Schwarzbauer. Munich: Musikverlag Bernd Katzbichler. Book and CD. 2013.

– *Akanthai: Orchestral and Ensemble Music*. Ensemble Modern, Nederlands Accordeon Ensemble, KNM Berlin, et al. CD. In preparation.

– *Autosymphonic: Open-Air Multimediasinfonie für Sinfonieorchester, 80 Automobile und 120 Perkussionisten, Chor, Kinderchor, Popband Vokalensemble, Perkussions-Oktett und Live Electronics*. SWR Sinfonieorchester Baden-Baden und Freiburg, Perkussions-Oktett des SWR Sinfonieorchester

Baden-Baden und Freiburg, SWR Vokalensemble Stuttgart, Kinderchor der Staatsoper Stuttgart, Söhne Mannheims, Xavier Naidoo. Conducted by Johannes Harneit, Klaas Stok and Johannes Knecht, Electronic sound production: Nick Elia, Staging: Horst Hamann. DVD. m:con–mannheim: congress GmbH, 2011.

- *Die Jagd: Naturoper mit Autos.* Stuttgart State Opera, Rampe Theatre Stuttgart, Stuttgart State Orchestra. Conducted by Bernhard Epstein, Staging: Eva Hosemann, Dramaturgy: Xavier Zuber. CD. Staatstheater Stuttgart, 2008.

- *Staubzucker.* Aesthis Records, EU, CD 0757450436070, 2015.

Europa 28 – Mit Marios Joannou Elia in Nicosia. Berlin: Deutsche Welle, Euromaxx – Leben und Kultur in Europa. July 7, 2013.

Gamelan & Kecak. produced and recorded by David Lewiston. CD. Warner, 2002.

Gespräch und Konzert: Adriana Hölszky im Gespräch mit Marios Joannou Elia. DVD. Akademie der Künste, Berlin, 2008.

Horizonte: Vor-Zeichen zur 9. Veranstaltung der musica viva – Marios Joannou Elia. Interview with Susanne Schmerda. Munich: Bayerischer Rundfunk – Klassik. August 31, 2009.

Insel der Dämonen. A film by Victor Baron von Plessen, Friedrich Dalsheim and Walter Spies. Dalsheim / Plessen Produktion, 1933.

Κυπραία Φωνή – Καλώς ήρταν οι ξένοι μας. 35 Traditional Songs of Cyprus. Double CD and CD Rom. Mousalyra, 2008.

Maori Haka and Chant: 25 Live Performances of Haka Groups Including the All Blacks Haka. CD. KMP Music, 2002.

Marios Joannou Elia at Entexnos. Interview with Alexia Karakanna and Elena Makri. Nicosia: Cyprus Broadcasting Corporation. March 22, 2012.

Motoren als Melodien, Hupen als Trompeten. Marios Joannou Elia in an interview with Uschi Goetz. Berlin: DeutschlandRadio Kultur. March 4, 2011.

Multimediales Gesamtkunstwerk für alle Sinne. Marios Joannou Elia in an interview with Horst Hamann, Eva Pinter, and Ulrich Erler. Mannheim: m:con visions, May 30, 2010.

Proust, Marcel. *Remembrance of Things Past*. Read by Neville Jason and Roy McMillan. 8 CDs. Naxos, 2010.

Wie geht das weiter mit der Musik? Marios Joannou Elia in an interview with Ursula Strubinsky. Vienna: Ö1 ORF, July 12, 2007.

Zeit-Ton – Portrait Marios Joannou Elia. Interview with Wolfgang Danzmayr. Vienna and Salzburg: Ö1 ORF, April 28, 2009.

3. Compositions[62]

Akanthai for chamber orchestra

Date: 2006

Instrumentation: flute, oboe, clarinet, bass clarinet, bassoon, horn, trumpet (2), trombone, percussion (2), piano, violin (I, II), viola, cello (I, II), double bass

Text: *The 9th of July 1821* by Vasilis Michaelides

Duration: 7'

Commission: Ensemble Modern, Allianz Cultural Foundation, Gesellschaft für Neue Musik (ISCM – German Section)

Premiere: House of the German Ensemble Academy, Frankfurt, February 18, 2007. Ensemble Modern, conducted by Stefan Asbury and Hsiao-Lin Liao

Akanthai for large orchestra

Date: 2006/09

Instrumentation: flute (3), oboe (3), clarinet (3), bassoon (3), horn (4), trumpet (3), trombone (3), percussion (3), piano, violin I (12), violin II (10), viola (8), cello (6), double bass (4)

Text: *The 9th of July 1821* by Vasilis Michaelides

Duration: 16'

Commission: German Radio Philharmonic Orchestra Saarbrücken – Kaiserslautern, Network Music Saar

Premiere: Mouvement – Festival for New Music, Great Broadcasting Hall of the Saarland Radio, May 21, 2009. German Radio Philharmonic Orchestra Saarbrücken – Kaiserslautern, conducted by Johannes Kalitzke

---

[62] This is a list of compositions mentioned in the commentary. A complete catalogue of works is available at http://www.mjelia.com; the Music Information Center Austria provides a list of works composed between 2001 and 2008.

Aquanauten for vocal ensemble

Date: 2007

Instrumentation: actors and/or singers (min. 5)

Text: *Odyssey* by Homer (twelfth song), *Dialectic of Enlightenment* by Max Horkheimer and Theodor W. Adorno, *Gadji beri bimba* and *Seepferdchen und Flugfische* by Hugo Ball

Duration: 25'

Commission: International Association for Polyaesthetic Education in Homage to Rector Professor Wolfgang Roscher

Premiere: Mirabell Palace Garden, Salzburg, October 18, 2007. Drama and Stage Directing Department of the Mozarteum University, Direction: Marios Joannou Elia

As Time Goes By – Zeitoper in three scenes

Date: 2005

Instrumentation: coloratura soprano, vocal ensemble (SATB), motorbike duet, spear carriers, flute, oboe, trumpet, horn, bassoon, trombone, percussion, violin, viola, cello, double bass

Libretto: *As time goes by* by Malte Ubenauf, Sven Holm, Xavier Zuber

Duration: 30'

Commission: Hannover State Opera

Premiere: Hannover State Opera, Hannover State Orchestra, Einsteinjahr 2005, September 29, 2005. Conductor: Johannes Harneit, Staging: Sven Holm

Autosymphonic – Open-air multimedia symphony for symphony orchestra, car orchestra (80 vehicles) and 120 car-players (120 percussionists), adult choir (8S-8A-8T-8B), children's choir, pop band vocal ensemble, percussion octet, electronics and 360-degree spatial sound reinforcement system

Date: 2010–11

Text: *Die Erfindung des Automobils. Erinnerungen eines Achtzigjährigen* by Carl Benz, *Im Auto über Land* by Erich Kästner, *Der Traum* by Xavier Naidoo and Metaphysics

Duration: 60'

Commission: City of Mannheim and m:con – mannheim:congress GmbH

Premiere: Closing celebration of the Automobile Summer Baden-Württemberg, Friedrichsplatz Square, Mannheim, September 10, 2011. SWR Baden-Baden and Freiburg Symphony Orchestra, SWR Vocal Ensemble Stuttgart, Stuttgart State Opera Children's Chorus, Söhne Mannheims, Pop Academy

Baden-Württemberg, 120 teenagers from the City of Mannheim, conducted by Johannes Harneit, Klaas Stok and Johannes Knecht, Electronic sound production: Nick Elia, Staging: Horst Hamann

Autotrio for automobile trio, 14 car-musicians and electronics

Date: 2010

Instrumentation: Benz Patent-Motorcar, Aero 6218R, Mercedes-Benz SLS AMG (or Audi R8 Spyder), 14 percussionists

Duration: 5'10"

Commission: City of Mannheim and m:con – mannheim:congress GmbH

Premiere: New Year's Reception of Mannheim's Mayor, Rosengarten Mozart Hall, Mannheim, January 6, 2011. Pop Academy Baden-Württemberg and National Theatre Mannheim, conducted by Harald Braun

Burning Motions – Staged concert in 12 scenes

Date: 2004

Instrumentation: six actors, piano, violin, viola, cello and electronics

Text: *Burning Motions* by Marios Joannou Elia

Duration: 65'

Commission: Arts Division of the Austrian Federal Chancellery, Mozarteum University of Salzburg

Premiere: International Mozarteum Foundation Salzburg, Wiener Saal, May 26, 2004. Departments of Drama – Thomas Bernhard Institute, Stage Design, Fine Arts, Art and Craft Education, ORFF-Institute for Elemental Music and Dance Pedagogy of the Mozarteum University, Actors: Michael Amelung, Ararat Chinarian, Robert Eder, Marios Joannou Elia, Jana Stefanek and Andy Kingston, Piano: Mario Sosa, Violin: Giorgos Manolas, Viola: Daniela Döhler, Cello: Gabriella Szabo, Direction: Marios Joannou Elia

Cicadas for amplified piano

Date: 2005

Text: *Die Zikaden* by Ingeborg Bachmann, *Zikaden* by Marios Joannou Elia

Duration: 5'

Commission: Cultural Funds of Land Salzburg

Premiere (short version): Vienna University of Music and Performing Arts, December 4, 2007. Piano: Eleni Papaspyrou

Premiere (long version): Avantgarde Tirol – Homage to Boguslaw Schaeffer, August 22, 2009. Piano: Slawomir Zubrzycki

Premiere with amplification: City University of New York, Lefrak Hall of Aaron Copland School of Music, November 17, 2011. Piano: Kristin Samadi

C Story for tenor, mixed western and non-western instruments

Date: 2006

Instrumentation: erhu, pan flute, recorder, qanum, viola da gamba, double bass, percussion (2)

Text: *Cyprus History* by Costas Montis

Duration: 6'

Commission: Ensemble Ziggurat, Amsterdam

Premiere: Gaudeamus Music Week, Amsterdam, September 8, 2006. Tenor: Bassem Alkhouri, Ensemble Ziggurat, conducted by Theo Leovendie/Joël Bons

Cursed for electric and classical guitar

Date: 2008

Duration: 8'

Commission: Arts Foundation Baden-Württemberg

Premiere: Republic – State of the Arts, Salzburg, May 17, 2008. Electric guitar: Ronny Wiesauer, Classical guitar: Kostas Tosidis

Das Geheimnis des Kleiderbügels – Staged concert in eight scenes

Date: 2005

Instrumentation: countertenor, two female singers and five actors, guitar (2), electric guitar (2), recorder, bassoon, trumpet, trombone, accordion, violin (3), cello, double bass, percussion (2)

Text: *Das Geheimnis des Kleiderbügels* by Marios Joannou Elia

Duration: 70'

Commission: Mozarteum Salzburg and Land Salzburg

Premiere: Toihaus Theatre Salzburg, June 10, 2005. Actors: Max Simonischek, Benjamin Bieber, Nina Mohr, Ulrich Rechenbach and Sara Spennemann, Countertenor: Philipp Caspari, Singer: Francka Senk and Jana Stefanek, Guitar: Giorgos Nousis, Cecilio Perera, Domenico Simone and Kostas Tosidis, Electric guitar: Gunter Wiesauer and Ronald Wiesauer, Recorder: Verena Huber, Bassoon: Sung-Min Kim, Trumpet: Johannes Bär, Trombone: Alex Moling, Accordion: Markus Schmid, Violin: Alessandro Calzavara,

Timea Ham, Giorgos Manolas, Ikuko Kitakado and Edson Scheid, Cello: Kristina Matcovic, Double bass: Tomoko Tadokoro, Percussion: Miwa Saeki and Yoko Yagihara, Conductor: Olga Mikhaleva, Staging: Susanne Inkiow, Scenery: Sandra Li Männel Saavedra and Thomas Mörschbacher, Direction: Marios Joannou Elia

Der Wegweiser for ensemble

Date: 2005

Instrumentation: flute, oboe, clarinet, bassoon, horn, percussion, violin (I, II), viola, cello, double bass

Text: *Winterreise* by Wilhelm Müller and *Ithaka* by Constantine Cavafy

Duration: 5'

Commission: European Cultural Year of the Ten, Berlin

Premiere: Berlin Philharmonic, May 27, 2005. Sinfonietta of Leipzig Gewandhaus Orchestra, conducted by Johannes Harneit

Die Jagd – Opera for nature and cars in 16 scenes

Date: 2008

Instrumentation: Maria I (coloratura soprano), Andy I (countertenor), Benni (boy soprano), Cem (Bass), Maria II (actress), Andy II (actor), Isabell (actress), juvenile vocal ensemble (hunting chorus), speaking choir, twenty voices (recorded or live), cello, accordion, harp, keyboards (one player for piano, cembalo, celesta and synthesizer), trumpet, horn, trombone, tuba, percussion (2), car sextet (Aston Martin DB9 Volante, Jaguar SKR, Ford Shelby Mustang, Ford Focus ST, Volvo S80, Land Rover Defender) and electronics

Libretto: *Die Jagd* by Marianne Freidig and Andreas Liebmann

Duration: 80'

Commission: Stuttgart State Opera

Premiere: Stuttgart State Opera, Rampe Theatre Stuttgart, Stuttgart State Orchestra, December 18, 2008. Conductor: Bernhard Epstein, Staging: Eva Hosemann, Dramaturgy: Xavier Zuber

Die Reise des G. Mastorna – Music theatre (media opera)

Date: 2006

Instrumentation: Conferencièse (actress), vocal ensemble (actors or singers), spear carriers, cello and guitar duet, Mexican mariachi quartet (violin, guitar, guitarron, male singer) and sound utensil ensemble

Libretto: *Die Reise des G. Mastorna* by Federico Fellini, arranged by Sandra Li Männel Saavedra and Marios Joannou Elia

Duration: 45'

Commission: Mozarteum Salzburg and City of Salzburg

Premiere: Amadeus Terminal 2 of the Salzburg Airport, Mozartjahr 2006 in Salzburg, October 25, 2006. Conferencièse: Ninja Reichert, With Johanna Baillet, Claudia Gaebel, Sebastian Graf, Elisabeth Halikiopoulos, Verena Jagersberger, Dennis Junge, Cello: Hugo Smit, Gitarre: Kostas Tosidis, Los Mariachis del Salzburg; Song: Rodrigo Porrus Garuto, Violin: David Varola López, Guitar: Francisco Torres, Guitarrón: Rafael Davila Troncoso, Mozarteum Department for Drama and Department for Stage Design, Costumes and video: Sandra Li Männel Saavedra, Direction: Marios Joannou Elia

Elpis for accordion orchestra

Date: 2006/07

Instrumentation: accordion (I, II, III, IV), electronium (I, II), bass accordion (I, II), percussion (2)

Text: *Hope Wanted* by Antonis Samarakis

Duration: 8'

Commission: Deutscher Harmonika Verband – DHV e. V.

Premiere: Harmo Novi, Trossingen – Festival for Contemporary Accordion

Elpis for accordion septet and percussion duet

Date: 2006/08

Instrumentation: accordion (5), electronium, bass accordion, percussion (2)

Text: *Elpis* by Antonis Samarakis

Duration: 8'

Commission: Hanne Darboven Foundation, Hamburg

Premiere: Gaudeamus Music Week, Amsterdam, September 2, 2008. Nederlands Accordeon Ensemble, Enschede, conducted by Egbert Spelde

En Plo for contrabass clarinet, double bass, electronics and loudspeaker orchestra

Date: 2007

Duration: 11'

Commission: Akademie der Künste, Berlin

Premiere: Plenarsaal of the Akademie der Künste, Berlin, December 1, 2007

Kammerensemble Neue Musik Berlin, Contrabass clarinet: Theo Nabicht, Double bass: Arnulf Ballhorn, Electronics: Nick Elia, AdK Studio for Electroacoustic Music Berlin

Holy Bread for amplified string quartet. Antidoron – Requiem for Costas Montis

Date: 2004

Instrumentation: violin solo and string trio

Text: *Moments of the Invasion* by Costas Montis, Paracelsus

Duration: 12'

Commission: stART Festival aktueller Musik, Salzburg

Premiere: Lutoslawski Festival, Warsaw Philharmonic, February 14, 2005. Rubinstein Quartet, Lodz

Premiere with amplification: Konzerthaus Berlin, June 18, 2006. Ensemble Modern, conducted by Titus Engel, Sound projection: Norbert Ommer

Hydor Chronos for electroacoustic music and video

Date: 2002/04

Text: *Chronogram* by Marios Joannou Elia

Duration: 14'

Commission: Cultural Funds of Land Salzburg

Premiere: House of the Mozarteum Orchestra, Salzburg, May 25, 2004. Video: Christoph Kendlbacher, Spatial sound projection: Marios Joannou Elia

Premiere in spatial modus: Salzburg Easter Festival, April 20, 2006

My Eyes, Only You for two actors

Date: 2002

Text: *My Eyes, Only You* by Marios Joannou Elia

Duration: 8'

Premiere: International Mozarteum Foundation Salzburg, Wiener Saal, June 14, 2002. Actors: Robert Eder, Michael Amelung

Refurbished – Staged concert in six scenes

Date: 2005

Instrumentation: countertenor, guitar (2), electric guitar (2), bassoon, trumpet, trombone, accordion, violin, cello, double bass, percussion

Text: *On tiptoe* by Marios Joannou Elia
Duration: 60'
Commission: Eliot Fisk's Guitar and Friends
Premiere: Central State Theatre Salzburg, April 24, 2005. Countertenor: Philipp Caspari, Guitar: Giorgos Nousis, Cecilio Perera, Domenico Simone and Kostas Tosidis, Electric guitar: Gunter Wiesauer and Ronald Wiesauer, Bassoon: Zhang Zhibai, Trumpet: Johannes Bär, Trombone: Alex Moling, Accordion: Olga Mikhaleva, Violin: Alessandro Calzavara, Giorgos Manolas and Edson Scheid, Cello: Kristina Matcovic, Double bass: Tomoko Tadokoro, Percussion: Mu Paopun Amnatham, Scenery: Sandra Li Männel Saavedra and Thomas Mörschbacher, Direction: Marios Joannou Elia

Staubzucker for guitar quartet
Date: 2007
Duration: 3'20"
Commission: International Association for Polyaesthetic Education in Homage to Rector Professor Wolfgang Roscher and Bankhaus Spraengler
Premiere: Solitär Salzburg, October 20, 2007. Miscelanea Guitar Quartet

Strophes for 11 vocal soloists, instrumental ensemble, loudspeaker ensemble and electronics
Date: 2003–04
Instrumentation: boy soprano, soprano (3), alto (2), tenor (2), bass (3), trumpet, tenor trombone, water horn, percussion (2), harp, conductor, assistant (actor/percussionist), sound director (2), car (VW Phaeton), elevator, glass tower, various sound equipment
Text: Ordinary of the Tridentine Mass, *Always for the First Time* by André Breton, *Médieuses*, *La Terre est Bleue* and *Premièrement* by Paul Eluard
Duration: 40'
Commission: The Volkswagen Transparent Factory and International Forum for Culture and Economy in Dresden

Tempus Tantum Nostrum Est for vocal ensemble S-A-T-B and motorbike duet
Date: 2005
Text: *Epistulae morales ad Lucilium 1* by Lucius Annaeus Seneca
Duration: 9'
Commission: Hannover State Opera, Deutsche Bank Stiftung

Premiere: Salzburg Biennale, March 6, 2009. Harley-Davidson Road King, Harley-Davidson Night Rod, Motodrom Salzburg, Ensemble Vocal Arts, Stuttgart, conducted by Angelika Luz

Tessera for recorder duet and double bass trio

Date: 2004

Text: Traditional folk song *Four and four*

Duration: 10'

Commission: Bank of Cyprus Cultural Foundation

Premiere: Orangerie Darmstadt, Internationale Ferienkurse, July 17, 2008. Recorder: Lisa Kortleitner, Verena Wüsthoff, Double bass: Dario Danone, Margarethe Maierhofer-Lischka, Fernando Yokota dos Santos, conducted by Eduardo Strausser, Uli Fussenegger and Jeremias Schwarzer

Thalatta, thalatta! for mandolin and ensemble

Date: 2007

Instrumentation: flute, clarinet, piano, violin, cello

Text: *Anabasis* by Xenophon

Duration: 8'

Commission: Klangspuren Schwaz

Premiere: Klangspuren Schwaz – Festival of Contemporary Music, Tyrol, September 8, 2007. Mandolin: Manuel de Roo, Austrian Ensemble for New Music

Totes Kleid for recorders and sewing machine

Date: 2005

Text: Traditional folk song *Four and four*

Duration: 5'

Commission: Mozarteum Salzburg

Premiere: Toihaus Theatre Salzburg, June 10, 2005. Recorders and sewing machine: Verena Huber

Vertumnus for electroacoustic music and interactive shadow play

Date: 2009

Duration: 40'

Commission: Republic of Cyprus – Ministry of Education and Culture

Supported by Skopje Biennale, Macedonian National Theatre, Association Biennale des Jeunes Créateurs de l'Europe et de la Méditerranée

Premiere: Skopje Biennale, September 9, 2009. Macedonian Opera and Ballet (big scene), Skopje

Whiteblack for baritone and ensemble

Date: 2003/05

Instrumentation: violin, guitar, percussion, trumpet, trombone

Text: *Turkish Invasion* by Costas Montis, newspaper reports

Duration: 15'

Commission: Eliot Fisk's Guitar and Friends, Salzburg

Premiere 1: Central State Theatre Salzburg. A portrait concert of works by Marios Joannou Elia. April 24, 2005

Premiere 2: Akademie Schloss Solitude, Stuttgart, June 15, 2012. Countertenor: Daniel Gloger, Ensemble Ascolta, conducted by Eva Fodor

www.ingramcontent.com/pod-product-compliance
Lightning Source LLC
Chambersburg PA
CBHW051616230426
43668CB00013B/2125